Skill Builders

A Grammar Workout

D1710229

Skill Builders

A Grammar Workout

Constance Immel
West Los Angeles College

Florence Sacks
West Los Angeles College

HarperCollins*College*Publishers

Acquisitions Editor: Mark Paluch
Development Editor: Marisa L. L'Heureux
Project Editor: Melonie Parnes
Design Supervisor: Mary Archondes
Cover Design: Delgado Design
Cover Photo: "The Swimmers," © Chris Harvey, Tony Stone Images
Production Administrator: Linda Greenberg
Compositor: Graphic Sciences Corporation
Printer and Binder: R.R. Donnelley & Sons Company
Cover Printer: The Lehigh Press, Inc.

Skill Builders: A Grammar Workout

93 94 95 96 9 8 7 6 5 4 3 2 1

Contents

Chapter 10   Usage   160

Preface

Skill Builders: A Grammar Workout is a workbook for students who have something to say but have difficulty saying it in standard English. We believe that the clearly worded definitions and examples, together with a variety of exercises, can help students in writing courses, in English-as-a-second-language classes, and in writing laboratories and tutor-assisted classes. We also believe that students can use this book on their own to brush up on rusty grammar skills.

To help students write clear, error-free sentences, the book features:

- Thorough coverage of key areas of grammar.
- Clear explanations with a minimum of grammatical terms.
- An abundant variety of exercises.
- An answer key at the end of the book to encourage students to work at their own pace and check their answers as they go.

We think that students learn best when they are actively engaged in the learning process. Therefore, we keep the explanatory material short, but we provide extensive examples and exercises that demonstrate the principle. Thus, the students are never faced with long, complicated explanations that are difficult to understand.

Many of the exercises are in paragraph form or contain sentences all on one topic. The topics are on subjects that should be of interest to students.

It is our hope that by using *Skill Builders: A Grammar Workout*, students will become competent writers by building their skills and confidence.

Constance Immel
Florence Sacks

1
Nouns and Pronouns

1.1 Identifying Nouns

If you were asked to give some examples of **nouns,** you probably would respond with words like astronaut, Mars, or spaceship. You would be right, because a noun does name a person, a place, or a thing, but a noun can also refer to an idea such as truth or an activity such as orbiting. A noun, then, names a person, a place, a thing, an idea, or an activity.

If you are not sure whether a word is a noun, put the word the in front of it. If the word is a noun, in most cases, the phrase will make sense. In addition to the, some other common noun markers are a, an, these, those, that, and this. A **noun marker** is an adjective that points to the noun that follows it: a car, the Washington Monument, that routine.

Common and Proper Nouns

All of the examples in the previous paragraph except the Washington Monument are **common nouns,** which refer to people, places, things, ideas, or activities in general terms. Common nouns are usually not capitalized except at the beginning of a sentence.

However, when we refer to the name of a specific person, place, or thing, we use **proper nouns,** which always begin with capital letters. In general we do not capitalize the names of ideas or activities. Using "the" as a noun test will not always help you identify proper nouns, but remembering that they are capitalized will help you pick them out.

Common Nouns	Proper Nouns
bridge	Vincent Thomas Bridge
woman	Yvonne Burke
street	Freshman Drive
college	Metropolitan Community College

EXERCISE 1.1

Using the noun test, identify the underlined words.

A. If the word is a noun, write N above the word.
B. If it is not a noun, write X above the word.

               N   X

Example: The clouds gathered before the storm.

1. The traffic on the highway stopped.

2. Rain fell last night.

3. Some drivers were cautious.

4. The surface of the road was slick.

5. John's Buick had good brakes.

Do not be confused by other words in addition to the noun marker that may be in front of the noun. These words that describe or limit the noun are also called **adjectives.** For example:

Noun Marker	Adj.	Noun	Noun Marker	Adj.	Noun
the	car	keys	this	new	typewriter

Adjectives answer questions such as <u>which</u> or <u>how many</u> in reference to a noun.

                                                                Adj. N

Example: the car keys   Which keys?   The <u>car</u> keys.

EXERCISE 1.2

Using the noun test, identify all the nouns in these sentences. Write N above each noun.

                   N   N   N

Example: Angela ate a large apple and a cheese sandwich.

Notice that the word <u>cheese</u> is not a noun in this sentence as it is in the sentence: <u>Joe likes cheese.</u> Angela is not eating plain cheese without any bread; she is eating a sandwich. <u>Cheese</u> tells us what kind of sandwich she is eating.

1. Mr. Cuadros gave us two free tickets to the basketball game.

2. Would you like a bowl of chicken soup and a fresh fruit salad?

3. I bought a digital watch for thirty dollars at K-Mart.

4. Lori wore a new green wool dress to her job interview.

5. The young doctor had a pleasant smile and a reassuring manner.

1.2   Singular and Plural Nouns

Use a **singular noun** when you are referring to only one person, place, thing, idea, or activity, and a **plural noun** when you are referring to more than one.

Noun Markers for the Singular

These words indicate that a singular word usually follows:

one	each
a	every
an	a single

Note: The noun marker **a** is followed by a word beginning with a consonant, and the noun marker **an** is followed by a word beginning with a vowel or a silent **h.**

Examples: a shoe   a home   an orange   an honor

Plural nouns present a special problem: Writing the singular form instead of the plural can change the meaning of your sentence. Study these basic rules for spelling the plural forms of nouns.

1. Most nouns form the plural by adding the letter **s.**

bed, beds   pen, pens   pipe, pipes

EXERCISE 1.3

Write the plural forms of these nouns.

1. dog _____

2. date _____

3. trick _____

4. test _____

5. sale _____

6. word _____

7. sentence _____

8. paragraph _____

9. operator _____

10. student _____

2. Words that end in **y,** preceded by a vowel **(a, e, i, o, u)** usually add **s** to form the plural. Words that end in **y,** preceded by a consonant, form the plural by changing the **y** to **i** and adding **es.**

city, cities   duty, duties   But note: bay, bays

2

EXERCISE 1.4

Write the plural forms of these nouns.

1. sky _____   6. turkey _____

2. day _____   7. county _____

3. lady _____   8. candy _____

4. penalty _____   9. army _____

5. key _____   10. battery _____

3. Words that end in **sh, s, ch, x,** and **z** form the plural by adding **es.**
   wish, wishes   church, churches,   buzz, buzzes

EXERCISE 1.5

Write the plural forms of these nouns.

1. brush _____   6. glass _____

2. watch _____   7. box _____

3. bus _____   8. mess _____

4. waltz _____   9. rash _____

5. tax _____   10. stitch _____

4. Nouns that end in **f, ff,** or **fe** usually add **s.** Certain nouns change the
   ending to **ve** and then add **s.** Consult your dictionary to be sure.

   knife, knives   loaf, loaves   calf, calves
   thief, thieves   roof, roofs   belief, beliefs
   proof, proofs   cliff, cliffs   staff, staffs

EXERCISE 1.6

Write the plural forms of these nouns.

1. self _____   6. life _____

2. half _____   7. thief _____

3. hoof _____   8. wolf _____

4. shelf _____   9. cliff _____

5. proof _____   10. wife _____

5. Most nouns ending in **o** form the plural by adding **s.** Here are six commonly used words, however, that are exceptions: echo, hero, potato, tomato, torpedo, and veto. To these words, add **es.**

   echo, echoes   hero, heroes   potato, potatoes

EXERCISE 1.7

Write the plural forms of these nouns.

1. soprano _____   6. radio _____

2. veto _____   7. zero _____

3. tomato _____   8. ratio _____

4. potato _____   9. hero _____

5. piano _____   10. domino _____

6. Some nouns do not add **s** or **es** to form the plural. These nouns change their spelling.

   woman, women   foot, feet   tooth, teeth
   goose, geese   child, children   mouse, mice

EXERCISE 1.8

Fill in each blank with the plural form of the noun in parentheses.

1. The children loved to play with the three white _____ (mouse).

2. We should have our _____ (tooth) examined twice a year.

3. Many _____ (woman) watch Monday-night football on television.

4. All of the _____ (child) in his family have gone to college.

5. There are five _____ (man) on the basketball court.

Noun Markers for the Plural

These words indicate that a plural word usually follows:

all	two (or more)	many	several	one of (the)
a lot of (the)	both	few		some
each of (the)		most		

1.3 Possessives

Making Nouns Possessive

In addition to nouns changing their forms to indicate the plural, nouns can change their forms to show ownership or a belonging-to relationship. To signal this relationship, we change the form of the noun by adding an apostrophe and the letter **s** or in some cases just the apostrophe.

Rules for Writing Possessive Nouns

1. Add an apostrophe and an **s** to words that do not end in **s**.

   the girl   the men   Linda
   the girl's scarf   the men's coats   Linda's pen

2. Add *only* an apostrophe to words that end in **s**.

   the girls   the monkeys   Mr. Harris
   the girls' scarves the monkeys' tails Mr. Harris' house

3. Add an apostrophe and an **s** to the final word in a compound noun.

   my father-in-law's business   somebody else's mistake

4. Add an apostrophe and an **s** to the second noun when two nouns are used to show common ownership.

   John and Gina's mother   Smith and Lopez's market

5. Generally the possessive form is not used with nonliving things.

   the table leg   the magazine cover

The following groups of words show a belonging-to relationship.

the trophy that belongs to the swimming team
the papers that belong to the students

But if you were writing about the trophy or the papers, you probably would use the possessive form of the noun.

The swimming *team's* trophy is on display.
The English teacher returned the *students'* papers.

EXERCISE 1.9

Rewrite the underlined words in the possessive form.

Example: The claws of the cats are sharp.   the cats' claws

© 1994 HarperCollins College Publishers

1. The <u>names of the cats</u> are Ginny and Max. _____

2. They listen to the <u>commands of their owners.</u> _____

3. They like to sleep in the <u>crib of the baby.</u> _____

4. The <u>mother of the baby</u> chases them out of the crib. _____

5. Sometimes Max tries to eat the <u>food that belongs to Ginny.</u> _____

Special Forms of the Possessive

Relationships other than possession are also shown by using the apostrophe and the letter **s.** Here are some examples:

time:	today's class	yesterday's visit
measure:	money's worth	two dollars' worth

EXERCISE 1.10

Put the apostrophe in each underlined noun to make it a possessive form.

1. Rain caused a cancellation of <u>Saturdays</u> game.

2. Jenny will be paid for two <u>weeks</u> vacation.

3. We will have a party on New <u>Years</u> Eve.

4. The employees have completed a good <u>days</u> work.

5. Where can you buy a <u>pennys</u> worth of candy?

Plurals and Possessives

Not every word ending in **s** requires an apostrophe. Most words ending in **s** are not possessive; many of them are noun plurals. The following exercise will give you practice using the plural and possessive forms of nouns. If necessary, review the rules given in this chapter on forming noun plurals and possessives.

EXERCISE 1.11

Add apostrophes to the possessive forms of the nouns in the following sentences. Some of the nouns are plural but not possessive and do not require apostrophes.

1. The Larsons visited friends in St. Paul.

2. Their friends house is near a lake.

3. On May 2, the refugees boat landed.

4. The refugees had only a few supplies with them.

5. Those dictionaries belong to the students.

6. I returned the students books to them.

7. Many customers were dissatisfied with the product.

8. Did the company refund the customers money?

9. When my car was being repaired, I used my parents car.

10. Many parents of the athletes attended the banquet.

1.4 Personal Pronouns

Pronouns are words that take the place of nouns and noun phrases. **Subject** and **object pronouns** act as the subject or object of a verb just as nouns do.

© 1994 HarperCollins College Publishers

The use of pronouns avoids the unnecessary repetition of nouns. Although pronouns perform the same functions in sentences as nouns do, you do not make the same changes in their forms. Do not add **s** for the plural and do not add an apostrophe in the possessive.

Person, Number, Gender

Personal pronouns show person, number, and gender. **Person** indicates the person speaking, the person spoken to, or the person or thing spoken about. See Chapter 3 for more on the use of pronouns.

>   **First person** shows the person speaking.
>   I mailed the letter.
>   We walked to the store.
>
>   **Second person** shows the person spoken to.
>   Did you mail the letter?
>   You are both invited to the party.
>
>   **Third person** shows the person or thing spoken about.
>   She shopped all day.
>   He wrapped and mailed the package.
>   It should arrive soon.
>   They enjoyed the play.

Avoiding Shifts in Person

Try to avoid unnecessary shifts from one person to another. These can confuse the reader. When writing about a person, choose one pronoun and stay with that pronoun.

The most common shift is to the pronoun you.

Incorrect: Most students can pass the tests my geology teacher gives if you study.

Correct: Most students can pass the tests my geology teacher gives if they study.

The noun students refers to third person; therefore, write they (third person) instead of you (second person). The pronoun should be in the same person as the noun it stands for.

Incorrect: When I shop for food, I check the price of each item that I put in the shopping cart. That way you know how much the bill will be when you get to the cashier.

Correct: The second sentence should read: That way I know how much the bill will be when I get to the cashier.

In the incorrect example, the writer has shifted from I (first person) to you (second person).

Some of the following sentences contain shifts in person. Identify each error by drawing a line under the pronoun; then write the correct form above the word. You may have to change the form of the verb.

                                              he or she

Example: When a person goes for a job interview, you should be well groomed.

1. I enjoy eating out instead of cooking at home. Living in Seattle, you have a choice of many different kinds of restaurants. My favorite restaurant is a Japanese one near my home. It is small and very popular, so you usually have to wait for a table.

2. If a person wants to learn to play a musical instrument well, you will have to develop self-discipline. The serious music student, for example, must be willing to give up watching two or three hours of television a day, and, instead, spend your time practicing.

© 1994 HarperCollins College Publishers

3. During the past year or two, the price of food has risen sharply. Every time I go to the market, you can see increases in several items. Not so long ago, your twenty dollars bought quite a few bags of groceries, but now I can carry twenty dollars' worth of food home in one bag.

4. I received a camera for a graduation present last year. It worked fine at first, but after a few months, you could tell that something was wrong with it. The pictures were so blurry that you couldn't recognize the people in them. The repairperson at the camera shop wanted too much money to repair it, so I stopped using it. You would be wasting your money to buy film for that lemon.

5. My brother likes his job as a lifeguard at the beach. You don't have to wear a coat and tie to work, and you are out in the fresh air all day. A lifeguard has an important job. You don't just watch pretty girls; you are responsible for the lives of all those people who come to enjoy the ocean.

Number indicates whether pronouns are singular or plural. Singular means one person or thing. Plural means more than one person or thing. Pronouns do not add **s** or **es** to form the plural.

Singular forms are used to refer to *one* person, thing, or idea.
I live in an apartment.
Don, have *you* met Carole?
She sent *it* to *her* mother.

Plural forms are used to refer to *more than one* person, thing, or idea.
Don't lose *them* again.
Three of *you* are tied for first place.
We have never met *their* son.

Third person pronouns have masculine, feminine, and neuter **gender.**

Third Person Pronouns

	MASCULINE		FEMININE		NEUTER	
	Singular	**Plural**	**Singular**	**Plural**	**Singular**	**Plural**
Subject	he	they	she	they	it	they
Object	him	them	her	them	it	them
Possessive	his	their	her	their	its	their

Possessive Pronouns—Short Forms (Use with Nouns)

Possessive pronouns are used to show possession or ownership.

Example: I washed <u>my</u> car.

In this sentence, I own the car; therefore, it is <u>my</u> car.

Person	**Singular**	**Plural**
First	my	our
Second	your	your
Third	his, her, its	their

In questions, use the pronoun **whose.**

Never add apostrophes to possessive pronouns.

Possessive Pronouns—Long Forms
(Use without Nouns)

Person	Singular	Plural
First	mine	our
Second	yours	yours
Third	his, hers	theirs

The long form of the possessive pronoun replaces the noun completely. We use the long form when the sentence follows another in which the noun is clearly stated.

Example: I washed my car. You didn't wash yours.

In these sentences, the reader should have no trouble understanding that yours replaces your car since the noun car is stated in the previous sentence.

EXERCISE 1.13

Rewrite the following pairs of sentences. Repeat the first sentence, but change the second one so that the underlined noun is not repeated. Use the long form of the possessive pronoun in place of the noun.

Example: This my pen. Your pen is in your pocket.

You write: This is my pen. Yours is in your pocket.

1. We like your car. The Palkas like their car too.

_____

2. Professor Wong teaches his classes in the morning. Professor Levy teaches her <u>classes</u> in the afternoon.

_____

3. Jerry carries his calculator in his pocket. Anna and Marlon carry their <u>calculators</u> in their briefcases.

_____

4. Aaron helps Rosa with her problems. No one helps Aaron with his <u>problems</u>.

_____

5. Your notebook is here on the desk. My <u>notebook</u> is in the car.

_____

The Pronoun <u>Who</u>

When used as the object of a verb or a preposition, the pronoun <u>who</u> has a special form—<u>whom</u>.

Examples: <u>Whom</u> do they recommend?
For <u>whom</u> did the city council vote?

Informal English accepts <u>who</u> rather than <u>whom</u>, except after a preposition. In conversation, most people would say, "<u>Who</u> do they recommend?"
   Also, remember the possessive form <u>whose</u> is used before a noun. Do not confuse it with the contraction <u>who's</u>, which replaces <u>who is</u>.

Contractions

In conversation and informal writing, the pronoun is often joined together with the verb that follows it. This is called a **contraction.** The two words are joined together with an apostrophe that takes the place of any missing letter.

Example: I am = I'm   you are = you're   it is = it's

Do not confuse the spelling of the possessive pronoun <u>your</u> with the contraction <u>you're</u>, or <u>its</u> with the contraction <u>it's</u>.

EXERCISE 1.14

Correct the spelling errors in the underlined pronoun forms.

1. <u>Your</u> moving to Oregon in a new van.   _____

2. <u>Their</u> parked in a no-parking zone.   _____

3. <u>Whose</u> going to the restaurant with us?   _____

4. <u>Its</u> too late to register for this class.   _____

5. <u>Their</u> playing my favorite song on the radio.   _____

6. Joanne gave Marsha her house key because Marsha   _____
   lost <u>her's</u>.

7. The Indians are leading in their division, and the   _____
   Braves are leading in <u>theirs'</u>.

8. My dog has learned to give me <u>it's</u> paw when I say,   _____

   "Give me <u>you're</u> paw."   _____

9. <u>Who's</u> dictionary may I borrow?   _____

10. <u>Your</u> going to pass this test on the first try.   _____

1.5   *Reflexive Pronouns*

Pronouns that end in **-self** and **-selves** are called **reflexive** pronouns.

Reflexive Pronouns

Singular I ←————————————————————— myself
you ←————————————————————— yourself
he ←————————————————————— himself
she ←————————————————————— herself
it ←————————————————————— itself

Plural we ←————————————————————— ourselves
you ←————————————————————— yourselves
they ←————————————————————— themselves

Do not write hisself, themself, or theirselves. These words are nonstandard English.

The reflexive pronoun is used in two ways:

   a.   I cut <u>myself</u>.

In sentence a, <u>myself</u> is used to refer back to <u>I</u>.

   b.   The president <u>himself</u> shook my father's hand.

In sentence b, <u>himself</u> is used to emphasize the person named, the president.
  Do not misuse reflexive pronouns by using them instead of personal pronouns in this way:

   c.   Gerry and <u>myself</u> went for a walk.

You would not write: <u>Myself</u> went for a walk. Use the subject form of the pronoun, I: Gerry and <u>I</u> went for a walk.

   d.   The Harts took Stan and <u>myself</u> sailing.

© 1994 HarperCollins College Publishers

You say: The Harts took <u>me</u> sailing, not <u>myself</u>. Use the object form of the pronoun, me: The Harts took Stan and <u>me</u> sailing. You can avoid making this error <u>by</u> using a reflexive pronoun only when it refers to another word in the sentence. Sentences c and d have no words for <u>myself</u> to refer back to.

If the use of the underlined reflexive pronoun is correct, write C on the line. If the use is not correct, write the correct pronoun.

1. He <u>himself</u> did all the work. _____

2. Laura and <u>myself</u> are science fiction fans. _____

3. We treated <u>ourselves</u> to large banana splits. _____

4. Give the plans to Mr. Zapata and <u>myself</u>. _____

5. They consider <u>themselves</u> experts. _____

Here is a chart of the pronouns you have studied in this chapter. Use it to help you remember the different kinds of pronouns we use in sentences.

Person	Subject Pronouns		Object Pronouns		Possessive Pronouns (With Nouns)		-s Form Possessive Pronouns (Without Nouns)	
	Singular	Plural	Singular	Plural	Singular	Plural	Singular	Plural
First	I	we	me	us	my	our	mine	ours
Second	you	you	you	you	your	your	yours	yours
Third	he	they	him	them	his	their	his	theirs
	she	they	her	them	her	their	hers	theirs
	it	they	it	them	its	their		

2

Verbs

2.1 Present and Past Tenses: Regular Verbs

Every sentence must have a **verb** to describe the action of the subject. Since the subject and the verb are the two most important parts of a sentence, learning to recognize verbs is essential to your progress in becoming a better writer. Let's review three characteristics of verbs that help to identify them.

1. The verb tells what the subject does, did, or will do (action), is, was, or will be (linking).

Example: Reggie caught the fly ball.
What did Reggie do?
He caught. Therefore, caught is the verb.

2. The verb changes its form to show time (tense).

Example: Reggie catches the fly ball. (The time is the present.)
Reggie caught the fly ball. (The time is the past.)
Reggie will catch the fly ball. (The time is the future.)

3. The verb changes its form in the third person singular, present tense to agree with the subject.

© 1994 HarperCollins College Publishers

Example: I catch the fly ball. (first person)
She/He catch<u>es</u> the fly ball. (third person)

There are two kinds of verbs: **action verbs** and **linking verbs.**

Action Verbs

Most verbs tell what the subject (someone or something) does, did, or will do. These **action verbs** are usually easy to identify, especially when the action is a familiar one, such as *swim, talk, buy, chew, study,* or *explode.*

Linking Verbs

Other verbs show a relationship between the subject and a completer that follows the subject. The completer usually describes or renames the subject, and the **linking verb** links the subject to this completer.

Subject	Linking Verb	Completer
Mr. Lopez	is	my Spanish teacher.
He	seems	tired.
Tacos	taste	good.

The linking verb used most frequently is some form of the verb *be (am, is are, was, were).* Some other linking verbs are *seem, grow, look, sound, taste,* and *appear.*

EXERCISE 2.1

In the following sentences, underline the verbs and write them on the lines at the right.

1. The train stops for only a few moments at Oakhurst.   _____

   The train stopped for only a few moments at Oakhurst.   _____

2. Gene hurries to get on the train already in motion.   _____

   Gene hurried to get on the train already in motion.   _____

3. He trips over a woman's suitcase in the aisle.   _____

   He tripped over a woman's suitcase in the aisle.   _____

4. Gene and the woman glare at each other.   _____

   Gene and the woman glared at each other.   _____

5. In his seat at last, he watches the dawn through the
   smeary windows of the train.   _____

   In his seat at last, he watched the dawn through the
   smeary windows of the train.   _____

The verbs in Exercise 2.1 form the past tense by adding -d or -ed to the base
form. Most verbs follow this pattern. These are called **regular verbs.**
   Verbs change their forms to indicate the time the action takes place. We
call this sign of time **tense.** The **present tense** is used in commands and sug-
gestions and to indicate habitual action or continuing ability.

Examples: Command: Deliver this message immediately.
           Suggestion: Discourage them from coming if you can.
           Habitual action: He paints beautifully.

Present progressive tense indicates that something is taking place right now
and may continue to occur for a while. The words now and right now often
indicate the use of the present progressive tense.

Examples: I am driving carefully.
           He is chopping the onions now.

The **past tense** is used in sentences about action that happened before the
present time. Say "Yesterday" at the beginning of the sentence to remind you
to use the past tense.

Example: Yesterday he chopped the onions for tonight's dinner.

© 1994 HarperCollins College Publishers

Here is a chart showing the pattern of the regular verbs in the present and the past tenses.

Model Verb—Walk

	Present Tense				Past Tense	
Person	**Singular**	**Plural**		**Person**	**Singular**	**Plural**
1st	I walk	we walk		1st	I walked	we walked
2nd	you walk	you walk		2nd	you walked	you walked
3rd	he walks	they walk		3rd	he walked	they walked
	she walks	they walk			she walked	they walked
	it walks	they walk			it walked	they walked

EXERCISE 2.2

Underline the verb in each of the following sentences. Write the present tense form of each verb on the line at the right.

1. Momoko planned a ski vacation in the mountains. _____

2. She worked extra hours at her job. _____

3. She saved half of her paycheck every week. _____

4. Momoko opened a special bank account. _____

5. She watched her money grow very slowly. _____

6. She waited for the first heavy snowfall. _____

7. She listened to the weather forecast every day. _____

8. Finally, the weather changed. _____

9. It snowed for three days and nights. _____

10. Momoko removed her money from the bank happily. _____

2.2 *Present and Past Tenses: Irregular Verbs*

Most verbs are regular verbs. We add **-d** or **-ed** to them to form the past tense. Verbs that do not add **-d** or **-ed** to form the past tense are called **irregular verbs.** Use your dictionary to find the past tense of irregular verbs or consult the chart of irregular verbs that follows.

Here is a chart listing some of the most commonly used irregular verbs.

Present (base form) Use with I, you, we, they, and plural nouns.	**Present + -s (-es)** Use with he, she, it, and singular nouns.	**Past** Use with all pronouns and nouns.	**Past Participle** Use with auxiliary verbs (has, had, have).	**Present Participle** Use with auxiliary verbs (is, am, are, was, were).
am, are	is	was, were	been	being
beat	beats	beat	beaten	beating
begin	begins	began	begun	beginning
bite	bites	bit	bitten	biting
blow	blows	blew	blown	blowing
break	breaks	broke	broken	breaking
bring	brings	brought	brought	bringing
burst	bursts	burst	burst	bursting
buy	buys	bought	bought	buying
choose	chooses	chose	chosen	choosing
come	comes	came	come	coming
dig	digs	dug	dug	digging
do	does	did	done	doing
draw	draws	drew	drawn	drawing
drink	drinks	drank	drunk	drinking
drive	drives	drove	driven	driving
eat	eats	ate	eaten	eating
fall	falls	fell	fallen	falling
fight	fights	fought	fought	fighting
find	finds	found	found	finding
fly	flies	flew	flown	flying
forget	forgets	forgot	forgotten	forgetting
freeze	freezes	froze	frozen	freezing
give	gives	gave	given	giving
go	goes	went	gone	going
grow	grows	grew	grown	growing

hang	hangs	hung	hung	hanging
have	has	had	had	having
hear	hears	heard	heard	hearing
hide	hides	hid	hidden	hiding
hold	holds	held	held	holding
know	knows	knew	known	knowing
lay	lays	laid	laid	laying
lie	lies	lay	lain	lying
lose	loses	lost	lost	losing
make	makes	made	made	making
ride	rides	rode	ridden	riding
ring	rings	rang	rung	ringing
rise	rises	rose	risen	rising
run	runs	ran	run	running
say	says	said	said	saying
see	sees	saw	seen	seeing
set	sets	set	set	setting
shake	shakes	shook	shaken	shaking
shine	shines	shone	shone	shining
sing	sings	sang	sung	singing
sink	sinks	sank	sunk	sinking
sit	sits	sat	sat	sitting
sleep	sleeps	slept	slept	sleeping
slide	slides	slid	slid	sliding
speak	speaks	spoke	spoken	speaking
spin	spins	spun	spun	spinning
stand	stands	stood	stood	standing
steal	steals	stole	stolen	stealing
stick	sticks	stuck	stuck	sticking
strike	strikes	struck	struck	striking
swear	swears	swore	sworn	swearing
swim	swims	swam	swum	swimming
swing	swings	swung	swung	swinging
take	takes	took	taken	taking
teach	teaches	taught	taught	teaching
tear	tears	tore	torn	tearing
throw	throws	threw	thrown	throwing
wake	wakes	waked	waked	waking
wear	wears	wore	worn	wearing
win	wins	won	won	winning
write	writes	wrote	written	writing

EXERCISE 2.3

All of the verbs in the following sentences are present tense forms of irregular verbs. Underline each verb. Then write the <u>past tense</u> form of each verb on the line at the right.

Example: The convention <u>begins</u> on Thursday.   began_____

1. Jugglers meet once a year at an international
   convention.   _____

2. They come from all age groups and many occupations.   _____

3. Each one gives a demonstration of his or her specialty.   _____

4. Everyone makes his or her presentation unique.   _____

5. These artists throw just about everything from cigar
   boxes to gold lamé beanbags up in the air.   _____

6. Some ride unicycles during their performances.   _____

7. One man even eats parts of an apple and a
   cucumber in his act.   _____

8. Jugglers have their names in the *Guinness Book of
   World Records.*   _____

9. Rastelli, an Italian juggler, still holds the record: ten
   balls or eight plates in motion at once.   _____

10. Amateur or professional, jugglers keep things on the
    move.   _____

2.3 *Principal Forms of Verbs*

When you change the spelling of a verb, you are changing the form of the verb. All verbs have five principal forms.

1. The **present or base form** is the verb without any changes in spelling. It is used with the pronouns I, you, we, and they and with plural nouns.

Examples: walk   see

2. The **present +s form** is spelled by adding an **-s** or **-es** to the base form. It is used with singular nouns and with the pronouns he, she, and it.

Examples: walks   sees

3. The **past form** is spelled by adding **-d** or **-ed** to a regular verb. Irregular verbs change the base form spelling in different ways. They should be memorized. The past form is used with all pronouns and nouns.

Examples: walked   saw

4. The **past participle** is spelled the same as the past form in regular verbs. Irregular verbs that change the spelling should be memorized. The past participle is used with a form of the auxiliary verb *have*.

Examples: has walked   has seen

5. The **present participle** is spelled by adding **-ing** to the base form of the verb. It is used with a form of the auxiliary verb *be*.

Examples: am walking   am seeing

All VERBS form the PRESENT PARTICIPLE by adding **-ing** to the PRESENT form:

Present	*Present Participle*	*Present*	*Present Participle*
walk	walking	try	trying

Some verbs, however, require a spelling change:

A. Drop a final, unpronounced **e** before adding a suffix beginning with a vowel.
   Examples: like, liking   use, using   come, coming
                  dine, dining
B. Double a final single consonant before a suffix beginning with a vowel:
   (1) if the consonant ends a stressed syllable or a word of one syllable, and
   (2) if the consonant is preceded by a single vowel.
   Examples: run, running   hop, hopping
                  begin, beginning   drag, dragging

EXERCISE 2.4

Add **-ing** to these words.

1. let _____

2. jump _____

3. hit _____

4. return _____

5. swim _____

6. occur _____

7. drip _____

8. wrap _____

9. scream _____

10. get _____

EXERCISE 2.5

Write the principal forms of the following regular verbs. Use your dictionary.

Present	Present + -s	Past	Past Participle	Present Participle
(base form) Use with I, you, we, they, and plural nouns.	Use with he, she, it, and singular nouns.	Use with all pronouns and nouns.	Use with auxiliary verbs (has, had, have).	Use with auxiliary verbs (is, are, am, was, were).

Example:

walk	walks	walked	walked	walking
1. stop				
2. carry				
3. watch				
4. try				
5. hope				

Principle Forms of Irregular Verbs

Unlike regular verbs, irregular verbs do *not* form their past and past participles by adding **-d** or **-ed** to the present form. Instead, they use some other change in form or they don't change at all:

  begin-began-begun   go-went-gone   set-set-set

EXERCISE 2.6

Write the principal forms of the following irregular verbs.

Present	Present + -s	Past	Past Participle	Present Participle
(base form) Use with I, you, we, they, and plural nouns.	Use with he, she, it, and singular nouns.	Use with all pronouns and nouns.	Use with auxiliary verbs (has, had, have).	Use with auxiliary verbs (is, are, am, was, were).

Example:

see	sees	saw	seen	seeing

1. am, are _____ _____ _____ _____

2. freeze _____ _____ _____ _____

3. run _____ _____ _____ _____

4. choose _____ _____ _____ _____

5. shake _____ _____ _____ _____

2.4 Auxiliary Verbs

An **auxiliary verb** is often added to the main verb to form the verb in a sentence. The present participle and the past participle forms are *not* used alone as the verb in a sentence. They are preceded by an auxiliary verb.

Example: Do not write: Thomas taking his brother to the park.

Do write: Thomas is taking his brother to the park.

© 1994 HarperCollins College Publishers

Note: When the verb phrase is underlined in this book, one line will indicate the auxiliary verb and two lines, the main verb. Example: will be speaking

The auxiliary verb has two main uses. First, the auxiliary verb indicates shades of meaning that cannot be expressed by a main verb alone.

He might go to college.   He can go to college.
He should go to college.   Would he go to college?

Second, the auxiliary verb indicates tense—the time the action of the verb takes place.

He is going to college.   He will go to college.
He has gone to college.   He does go to college.

Note that in a question, the subject separates the auxiliary verb and the main verb.

Will he go to college?

Auxiliary verbs are commonly divided into two groups.

Group 1: The following words are used with main verbs, but they are *not* used as verbs alone except in answer to a question. They *signal* the approach of a main verb.

can	may	shall	will	must
could	might	should	would	ought (to)

EXERCISE 2.7

Underline the auxiliary verb once and the main verb twice. There may be more than one auxiliary verb.

Example: I would like to place an order.

1. Do you shop at home?

2. You might have received a mail-order catalog from time to time.

3. Many people have found these catalogs convenient.

4. Years ago, farm families could send for clothes and household needs.

5. Today, urban shoppers can order a variety of goods from specialty stores.

Group 2: The following verbs may be used as auxiliary verbs or as main verbs. When they serve as auxiliaries, another form of a verb is used as the main verb of the verb phrase.

be	am	have	do
being	is, are	has	does
been	was, were	had	did

Remember

1. A sentence must always have a main verb, but it may or may not have an auxiliary verb.

2. If the sentence has an auxiliary verb, it is always placed in front of the main verb.

3. In a question, the subject separates the auxiliary verb and the main verb.

EXERCISE 2.8

In the following sentences, underline the auxiliary verb or verbs once and the main verb twice. Do not underline the contraction for *not (n't)*.

Example: I <u>didn't</u> <u>understand</u> the question.

1. Many injured athletes have been helped by a new instrument called an arthroscope.

2. With the arthroscope, doctors can see inside the knee.

3. The doctor can examine bones and tissues.

4. The surgery may be done within an hour.

5. Without the arthroscope, a doctor must cut open the knee.

Summary

1. Present and past participles must be accompanied by an auxiliary verb.

2. Present and past participles cannot function alone as the verbs of a sentence.

3. *Be, have,* and *do* sometimes function as auxiliary verbs.

   I have finished my homework.   I didn't speak to him.   I was eating.

4. *Be, have,* and *do* often function alone in a sentence as main verbs.

   I have a penny.   I do my homework.   I was an only child.

EXERCISE 2.9

Fill in the correct form of the main verb in parentheses to complete the sentence. Consult the chart of irregular verbs or your dictionary.

1. (run) Since his father's death, Nick has _____ the family business.

2. (sing) Our college chorus has _____ at the Music Center before.

3. (see) We have _____ that movie twice.

4. (hear) Have you _____ the results of the election yet?

5. (break) Lee has _____ his promise again.

6. (know) How long have you _____ Liang Wong?

7. (fly) The pilot had _____ helicopters over Vietnam before he came to the United States.

8. (bring) The letter carrier has _____ the mail early today.

9. (eat) We had never _____ at that restaurant before we tried it last week.

10. (say) What has Vince _____ about his trip to Japan?

Adverbs

An **adverb** is a modifier that adds further information about verbs, adjectives, and other adverbs. The following adverbs, in addition to others, frequently appear between auxiliary verbs and main verbs. These words are not auxiliary verbs. Do not underline them as verbs.

never	always	often	sometimes
not	still	seldom	completely
just	ever	frequently	

Examples: Television will **never completely** replace the radio.
            The football game has **just** ended.

Contractions

In conversation and informal writing, two words are often joined together with an apostrophe that takes the place of any missing letters. The contraction for not (n't) may be added to many auxiliaries, for example:

haven't   doesn't   aren't   can't   isn't   won't

Note: *n't* is not an auxiliary verb; do not underline it as one.

Examples: We hadn't seen them for years.
            The mechanic couldn't repair the car in one day.

EXERCISE 2.10

In the following sentences, underline the auxiliary verb or verbs once and the main verb twice. Put parentheses around any adverbs or contractions.

Example: Cassandra <u>does</u>(n't) <u><u>smoke</u></u> cigarettes any longer.

1. Dr. Dimaio isn't in her office today.

2. You should always practice your scales.

3. My boss must certainly give me a raise.

4. Tim may travel to New Orleans next month.

5. Could you close the window for me?

2.5 Future Tense

The **future tense** is used for sentences about something that will happen in the future. The future tense is formed by using the auxiliary verbs <u>will</u> or <u>would</u> and the base form of the main verb. Here is a chart showing the pattern of all verbs in the future tense.

Model Verb—Walk			
Person	**Singular**	**Person**	**Plural**
1st	I will walk	1st	we will walk
2nd	you will walk	2nd	you will walk
3rd	he will walk	3rd	they will walk
	she will walk		they will walk
	it will walk		they will walk

Although it is correct to express future action by using the present pro-gressive tense (I **am going** to graduate in June.), use only the future tense (I **will graduate** in June.) when you are writing the exercises in this lesson.

EXERCISE 2.11

Complete the following sentences by using the future tense of the verb in the parentheses.

1. (want) Tomorrow Tom _____ your car.

2. (earn) Tomorrow I _____ my first paycheck.

3. (begin) Next week Linda _____ her new job.

4. (stay) From now on Jan _____ home in the evenings.

5. (ask) I hope he _____ me for a date this afternoon.

Will and Would

Will points to the future from the present.   **know/will**
Would points to the future from the past.   **knew/would**

    a. You <u>know</u> that you <u>will</u> do well in this class.

In sentence a, "you know" <u>now</u> (in the present) that "you will do well" in the <u>future</u>.

    b. You <u>knew</u> that you <u>would</u> do well in this class.

In sentence b, "you knew" <u>then</u> (in the past) that "you would do well" in the <u>future</u>.

© 1994 HarperCollins College Publishers

EXERCISE 2.12

In the following sentences, fill in <u>will</u> or <u>would</u> to indicate the future.

1. Herb knows that he _____ win someday.

2. Herb knew that he _____ win someday.

3. Wu arrives early so he _____ get the best seats.

4. Wu arrived early so he _____ get the best seats.

5. He says that he _____ hire a band.

6. He said that he _____ hire a band.

2.6 *Perfect Tenses*

In the lesson on auxiliary verbs, you used the perfect tenses in some of the verbs that you identified or wrote. The name **perfect tenses** gives no clue to the uses of these tenses. Study the following examples to learn how to use the perfect tenses.

A. The **present perfect tense** is formed by using the auxiliary verb **have** in the present tense plus the past participle of the main verb.

Model Verb—Run			
Person	**Singular**	**Person**	**Plural**
1st	I have run	1st	we have run
2nd	you have run	2nd	you have run
3rd	he has run	3rd	they have run
	she has run		they have run
	it has run		they have run

Use the present perfect tense to show that an action began in the past and has continued until now, or that an action has just happened. It is often used to show that an action occurred at an indefinite time in the past. Adverbs such as *just* and *already* are commonly included.

EXERCISE 2.13

Fill in the present perfect tense of the verb given in the parentheses. Use the chart of irregular verbs or your dictionary.

Example: Mike has seen all the home games of the Dallas Cowboys this season.

1. (predict) The weatherman _____ just _____ snow for the weekend.

2. (keep) We _____ _____ the puppies in our backyard for two months.

3. (plan) What kind of food _____ you _____ to serve this evening?

4. (bring) The students _____ _____ their dictionaries to class for the past two sessions.

5. (buy) They _____ _____ their groceries at the same store for many years.

B. The **past perfect tense** is formed by using the auxiliary verb **had** plus the past participle of the main verb.

Model Verb—Run			
Person	**Singular**	**Person**	**Plural**
1st	I had run	1st	we had run
2nd	you had run	2nd	you had run
3rd	he had run	3rd	they had run
	she had run		they had run
	it had run		they had run

Use the past perfect tense to show that one action happened before another action in the past. Use it only when you are writing in the past tense.

Fill in the past perfect tense of the verb given in parentheses. Use the chart of irregular verbs or your dictionary.

Example: After we <u>had</u> <u>seen</u> the play, we went to a restaurant for dessert.

1. (show) The nurse _____ _____ me how to diaper the baby before she left.

2. (promise) Darrell _____ _____ to love her when they got married.

3. (have) Antonio _____ _____ an excellent job in New Orleans before he moved to Houston.

4. (run) The dog _____ _____ after the cat until the cat climbed a tree.

5. (choose) We _____ _____ this book before we looked at the others.

C. The **future perfect tense** is formed by using the auxiliary verbs **will have** plus the past participle of the main verb.

Model Verb—Run

Person	Singular	Person	Plural
1st	I will have run	1st	we will have run
2nd	you will have run	2nd	you will have run
3rd	he will have run	3rd	they will have run
	she will have run		they will have run
	it will have run		they will have run

Use the future perfect tense to show that something will happen in the future by a specific time.

EXERCISE 2.15

Fill in the future perfect tense of the verb given in parentheses. Use the chart of irregular verbs or your dictionary.

Example: By the time her trip is over, Anita <u>will</u> <u>have</u> <u>seen</u> every state in the United States.

1. (learn) By this time next week, you ＿＿＿＿＿ ＿＿＿＿＿

    ＿＿＿＿＿ how to drive a car.

2. (pay) By this time next year, Paul ＿＿＿＿＿ ＿＿＿＿＿

    ＿＿＿＿＿ for the car.

3. (live) By next June they ＿＿＿＿＿ ＿＿＿＿＿

    ＿＿＿＿＿ in that house for twenty years.

4. (go) By September I ＿＿＿＿＿ ＿＿＿＿＿ ＿＿＿＿＿
    to college for two years.

5. (speak) By election day the candidate ＿＿＿＿＿ ＿＿＿＿＿

    ＿＿＿＿＿ at ninety meetings.

2.7 Tense Shift Problems

Do *not* shift tenses in the middle of a sentence, a paragraph, or an essay unless you have a reason to do so. If you begin writing in the present tense, don't shift to the past. If you begin in the past, don't shift to the present.

© 1994 HarperCollins College Publishers

Incorrect: Kite flying *is* a good way to meet people. They *were* curious when they *saw* my kite up there. They *wonder* why I *waste* my time with a kite.

Shifts from present to past tense and back to present tense.

Correct: Kite flying *is* a good way to meet people. They *are* curious when they *see* my kite up there. They *wonder* why I *waste* my time with a kite.

All the verbs are in the present tense.

Correct: Kite flying *was* a good way to meet people. They *were* curious when they *saw* my kite up there. They *wondered* why I *wasted* my time with a kite.

All the verbs are in the past tense.

EXERCISE 2.16

Some of the following sentences contain shifts in tense. Identify each error by drawing a line under the incorrect verb. Write the correct form above the word.

Example: The rain began when we s̲t̲e̲p̲ off the bus. [stepped]

1. Last Tuesday night I went to the library because I had a test in history on Wednesday morning. It is too noisy at home to study. My brother is playing the stereo, my mother was vacuuming, and my little sister and her friend are chasing each other around the house. How am I supposed to concentrate with all that commotion?

2. My friend Greg loves peanut butter. Every morning he spread peanut butter on his toast or waffles. He snacked on peanut butter cups at school, and, of course, he ate peanut butter sandwiches for lunch every day. Now-

adays he bakes his own peanut butter cookies because his mother had refused to make them anymore. Greg was a hopeless case; he even covers a slice of chocolate cake with peanut butter.

3. My wife and I bought a golden retriever puppy last year. We made the mistake on the first few nights of allowing the puppy to sleep on a rug by our bed because he misses his brothers and sisters. Later when we made a bed for him in the laundry room, he howls and scratches on the door for several hours every night. After a while the neighbors call on the telephone to complain about the noise. We thought that he will never give up. The puppy finally learned to sleep by himself, and the neighbors start speaking to us again.

© 1994 HarperCollins College Publishers

3

The Sentence

3.1 Subjects and Verbs

The **subject** of a sentence is the person or the thing the **verb** is asking or telling about. The subject may be a **noun** or a **pronoun.** Every sentence must have at least one subject and one verb and express a complete thought.

Example: The tourists <u>have</u> <u>returned</u> home. Subject = tourists.
To find the subject ask, "Who <u>have</u> <u>returned</u> home?" The answer, "The tourists," is the subject.

Finding Subjects and Verbs

1. First, find the verb. Underline the auxiliary verb once and the main verb twice.

   Fish <u>swim</u>.   They <u>can</u> <u>play</u>.

2. Then, find the noun or pronoun subject by asking <u>who</u> or <u>what</u> with the verb. Circle the subject.

   What <u>swim</u>? (Fish) <u>swim</u>.   Who <u>can</u> <u>play</u>? (They) <u>can</u> <u>play</u>.

   The answer gives you the noun or pronoun subject circled previously.

(continued)

3. If the sentence asks a question, put the sentence in the form of a statement to help you find the subject and the verb.

Are the children playing? Change to: The children are playing.

Then ask: Who are playing?

The answer gives you the subject. The (children) are playing.

4. Remember that every sentence must have at least one subject and one verb.

EXERCISE 3.1

Underline the auxiliary verb once and the main verb twice. Circle the subject. The last sentence has more than one subject and verb.

Example: Has the (letter) arrived yet?

1. Does a Scotsman wear anything under his kilt?

2. Americans can satisfy their curiosity without a trip to the Highland Games in Scotland.

3. Similar festivals are held in the United States each year.

4. The numerous events include many tests of strength, such as contests for shot putters, hammer throwers, and caber (pole) tossers.

5. During the caber toss, the contestants are throwing 100-pound, eighteen-foot poles with remarkable balance and accuracy.

Commands and Requests

Each sentence must have at least one subject and one verb, but the verb can stand alone in a sentence without a stated subject in a **command** or **request.**

© 1994 HarperCollins College Publishers

The subject in such a sentence is "**you, understood.**" In other words, it is understood that the subject is "you."

Examples:

$$\underline{\underline{\text{Look!}}} = \overset{\text{S}}{\bigcirc\!\!\!\!\text{You}} \underset{\text{V}}{\underline{\underline{\text{look!}}}}$$

$$\underline{\underline{\text{Hurry!}}} = \overset{\text{S}}{\bigcirc\!\!\!\!\text{You}} \underset{\text{V}}{\underline{\underline{\text{hurry!}}}}$$

EXERCISE 3.2

Fill in the blanks with verbs that command or request.

1. _____ to the party tomorrow.

2. _____ your name here.

3. _____ the door.

4. _____ me here after class.

5. _____ a glass of punch.

3.2   Prepositional Phrases

Not many sentences have subjects and verbs as easy to recognize as those in the sentences you have been working with. We usually add words to the subject and the verb to give more information about them. Sometimes we use one word, sometimes a group of words. A group of words introduced by a preposition and known as a **prepositional phrase** is often used to expand the subject and the verb.

Prepositions are the short words that show position, relationship, or direction. For example, if you were trying to give the location of your pencil, you might say: The pencil is on the desk. Or, the pencil is under the desk. The prepositions are on and under. The prepositional phrases are on the desk and under the desk.

Each prepositional phrase contains at least two words: a **preposition** (P) and an **object** (O). The object (O) is always a noun or a pronoun.

<pre>
                 S   P   O
</pre>
Example: Lloyd <u>enjoys</u> a glass of root beer.

Some prepositional phrases contain adjectives that come between the preposition and the object. These words describe the object.

<pre>
                 S   P Adj   Adj   O
</pre>
Example: Lloyd <u>enjoys</u> a glass of cool, foamy beer.

Commonly Used Prepositions

Position	Direction	Relationship
about	at	as
above	beyond	because of
across	down	but
after	from	by
against	in	except
along	into	for
before	on	like
during	to	of
near	toward	since
until	up	with

In this chapter bracket ([]) all prepositional phrases in sentences to help locate the subjects and verbs of the sentences. The main reason for learning to recognize prepositional phrases is to help find the subject and the verb of a sentence. One common mistake in identifying the subject of a sentence is confusing it with a noun used as the object of the preposition. Any word that is part of the prepositional phrase *cannot* be the subject of the sentence.

EXERCISE 3.3

Bracket all the prepositional phrases in the following sentences. Use the chart to help you identify the prepositions.

© 1994 HarperCollins College Publishers

Example: Many young Americans work [in Washington, D.C.]

1. Since 1789 young Americans between the ages of fourteen and eighteen have served as congressional pages in our nation's capital.

2. Some work during vacation while others leave their families and friends to live in Washington, D.C., for a year, continuing high school classes at Page School in the Library of Congress.

3. A page delivers mail, answers telephone calls, and runs errands for members of Congress from 9 A.M. to 5 P.M.

4. Not all legislators approve of the present system. One senator believes that the pages' work is demeaning and that they should be at home with their parents.

5. Most pages would not agree, for despite the pressures of a busy schedule, they enjoy their work and the excitement of national political life.

Prepositions of Two or More Words

These prepositions are made up of two or more words as in the sentence:
I made the cake according to those directions.

according to	in addition to	in spite of
along with	in case of	on account of
because of	in front of	on top of
by means of	in the middle of	out of
contrary to	in place of	together with
for the sake of	instead of	with reference to

EXERCISE 3.4

Bracket all the prepositional phrases in the following sentences. Use the lists given earlier to help you identify the prepositions.

Example: [In the middle of the night,] the telephone rang.

1. The rack on top of the car will hold our skis and several pieces of luggage.

2. Instead of a salad, Kevin prefers soup with his dinner.

3. The man in front of me complained about the long wait in line.

4. After two innings, the baseball game at Yankee Stadium was called because of rain.

5. The mayor, together with several council members, participated in a panel discussion on the city's transit problems.

3.3   Direct Objects of Action Verbs

Some action verbs may be followed by a **direct object** to complete the meaning of the sentence. To find the direct object of the verb, place <u>what</u> or <u>whom</u> after the subject and the verb.

Finding the Direct Object of the Verb

1. Gail's bicycle needs a new tire.
              S   V

2. Ask: "Gail's bicycle needs what?"
                  S   V   O

3. The answer is: "Gail's bicycle needs a new tire."

4. Therefore, the noun <u>tire</u> is the object.

© 1994 HarperCollins College Publishers

EXERCISE 3.5

A. Place brackets around the prepositional phrases.
B. Write the word that is the direct object of the verb on the line at the right. If there is no object, leave the space blank.

Direct Object

S

Example: Do (you) want some coffee [for lunch]?   coffee

1. My uncle plays for the Dodgers.   _____

2. The children asked many questions today.   _____

3. Did you order food from the deli?   _____

4. Marilyn sang in the choir last year.   _____

5. Can Steve play the guitar?   _____

3.4 Linking Verbs

Action verbs tell what the subject does, did, or will do.

Linking verbs do *not* tell what the subject does. Linking verbs are verbs of being. They include all forms of the verb be—am, is, are, was, were, been, and being—and other verbs such as seem, feel, become, and appear, which can be substituted for forms of be. Linking verbs link the subject with another word in the sentence that is called the **completer.**

1. The verb links the subject to a noun completer that *renames* the subject.

            S   NC   S   NC

Examples: Judi is a *dancer.*   Mr. Bradley is our football *coach.*

2. The verb links the subject to an adjective completer that *describes* the subject.

           S   AC   S   AC

Examples: Judi is *graceful*.   Mr. Bradley is *enthusiastic*.

Linking Verbs

appear	become	grow	remain	taste
be	feel	look	seem	turn

In the following examples, S = subject and C = completer.

         S   C

1. The velvet feels soft.

         S   C

2. Has this milk turned sour?

         S   C

3. Nevertheless, she will remain our president.

    S   C

4. Darrell had become a pole vaulter in college.

                   S   C

5. On the surface, the coach's decision seemed reasonable.

Some of these linking verbs can also be used as action verbs. When used as action verbs, they may be followed by direct objects. They may also be used as action verbs without direct objects. Study these examples:

Linking Verbs

        S   LV C

a. The corn grows tall.

        S   LV   C

b. The cake tasted delicious.

         S   LV   C

c. The patient appeared better.

Action Verbs

        S   V   O

d. The farmer grows corn.

        S   V   O

e. Marla tasted the cheesecake.

      S————————S

f. Richard and Elizabeth

            V

appeared in a play together.

© 1994 HarperCollins College Publishers

In sentences d and e, the action verbs are followed by direct objects. In sentence f, the action verb is not followed by a direct object. Remember that these verbs are linking verbs only when they are followed by a word or phrase that renames or describes the subject of the sentence, as in sentences a, b, and c.

EXERCISE 3.6

Circle the subject, underline the auxiliary and the main verbs, and label the completer in each of the following sentences.

Examples: The (mango) is a tropical fruit.

This (mango) looks ripe.

1. My daughter is a first-year student at Jackson Community College.

2. Everyone seemed happy about the election results.

3. The traffic light is finally turning green.

4. Mario and Kevin have just become partners.

5. Can you be the moderator of our next discussion?

3.5 Pronouns Used as Subjects and Objects

Subject Pronouns

Subject pronouns are used primarily as the subjects of sentences or clauses. They also are used after all forms of the verb be in formal writing.

Example: It is I. (In conversation, most people would say, "It's me.")

Subject Pronouns

Person	Singular	Plural
First	I	we
Second	you	you
Third	he, she, it	they

EXERCISE 3.7

Referring to the forms in the box above, underline the subject pronouns in the following sentences.

Example: <u>They</u> enjoy bowling because <u>it</u> is good exercise.

1. He removed the tire because it was flat.

2. Have you seen Pat since she returned from Chicago?

3. As parents, you will be interested in this program we are proposing.

4. They read the instructions carefully.

5. Every Saturday I play tennis.

Object Pronouns

Object pronouns have two main uses: as objects of verbs and as objects of prepositions. As the objects of verbs, they usually follow the verbs.

           V   Noun Object   V   Pronoun Object

The outfielder caught the *ball*.   The outfielder caught *it*.

Object pronouns can also be objects of prepositions, words such as <u>in</u>, <u>to</u>, <u>with</u>, and <u>for</u>:

Prep. Noun Object   Prep. Pronoun Object

Shana gave a party for *Donna*.   Shana gave a party for *her*.

© 1994 HarperCollins College Publishers

Objects always follow the preposition:

to <u>me</u>   with <u>you</u>   in <u>it</u>   for <u>us</u>   without <u>them</u>

Object Pronouns		
Person	**Singular**	**Plural**
First	me	us
Second	you	you
Third	him, her, it	them

EXERCISE 3.8

Referring to the forms in the box, underline the object pronouns in the following sentences.

Example: The coach gave the awards to <u>him</u>.

1. The stereo is too loud; turn it down.

2. Eduardo met us at Disney World.

3. Terry will wait for her.

4. Did Todd tell you about them?

5. The news pleased me.

3.6 Compound Subjects, Verbs, and Objects

Until now, most of the sentences in this book have contained simple subjects and simple verbs. Many sentences, however, have **compound subjects** and **compound verbs**. A compound subject is made up of two or more subjects joined by coordinating connectives, such as <u>and</u> or <u>or</u>. A compound verb is made up of two or more verbs joined by coordinating connectives, such as <u>and</u> or <u>or</u>.

Simple Subject

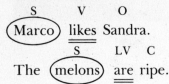

Compound Subject

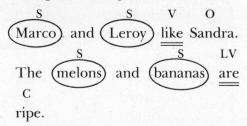

Simple Verb

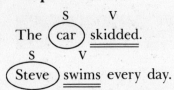

Compound Verb

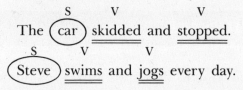

Objects and completers can also be compound.

Compound Object

S   V   O   O   O
(She) brought fresh beans, squash, and tomatoes from her garden.

Compound Completer

S LV   C   C
(He) is an actor and a musician.

          S   LV C   C   C
The (colors) of her dress are red, white and blue.

Pronouns in Compound Subjects and Objects

Compound subjects and objects can be a problem when they include pronouns. For example, what pronouns would you place in these blanks?

© 1994 HarperCollins College Publishers

1. Bob and _____ (me, I) went to the game Friday.
2. We waited for Tom and _____ (he, him) after class.

I is correct in sentence 1 because I is the subject of the verb. Him is correct in sentence 2 because him is the object of the preposition for.

When you are in doubt about the form of a pronoun in sentences like these, leave out the noun subject or the noun object and the connective and read the sentence with the pronoun by itself.

1. Bob and I went to the game Friday. (You read, "I went to the game Friday" because you wouldn't say, "Me went to the game Friday.")
2. We waited for Tom and him after class. (You read, "We waited for him after class" because you wouldn't say, "We waited for he after class.")

Sometimes you might have to change the sentence slightly:

Bob and _____ (me, I) have been friends for years.
Change to: I have been Bob's friend for years.

EXERCISE 3.9

Underline the correct pronoun.

Example: My brother and (I, me) want to buy a condominium together.

1. We want to find one that has a bedroom for (he, him) and one for me.

2. (He, Him) and (I, me) have been sharing one bedroom for a long time.

3. There has never been any trouble between (we, us).

4. The real estate agent asked whether my brother and (I, me) need two bathrooms.

5. My brother said that (he, him) and (I, me) need two bedrooms and two bathrooms.

3.7 *Contractions*

You learned that the contraction for not (n't) may be added to many auxiliary verbs (do not = don't; does not = doesn't). Contractions may also be formed by combining pronoun subjects and verbs. In writing contractions, do not omit the apostrophe. Note in the following examples that the apostrophe replaces the letter or the letters that have been omitted.

Omitting Letters in a Verb

Examples: She is my sister. She's my sister:
She will have to explain. She'll have to explain.

In each of these examples, a pronoun (she) and a verb (is, will) have been combined. The apostrophe takes the place of the letter i in is and the letters wi in will. She is = she's; she will = she'll.

Omitting the i in Here is and There is

Contractions may also be formed by combining there with is and here with is.

Examples: There is John now. There's John now.
Here is your book. Here's your book.

In both cases the apostrophe takes the place of the letter i in is. Note: There are and here are are never contracted. Furthermore, when a sentence begins with the words here is or there is, the noun that follows the verb is the subject.

EXERCISE 3.10

Supply the contractions for these words.

1. she will   she'll   6. I am   _____

2. they have   _____   7. we have   _____

3. he had   _____   8. here is   _____

4. he is   _____   9. it is   _____

5. I will   _____   10. we are   _____

3.8 Sentence Patterns

There are four basic sentence patterns.

Pattern 1 Subject-Verb (S-V) Sentences following this pattern may have only a subject and a verb:

       S   V   S   V   S   AV   V
    a. People travel.   b. Planes landed.   c. They had arrived.

This pattern, of course, can have compound subjects and/or verbs:

       S   S   V   S   V   V
    d. Elaine and Allen sang.   e. The audience clapped and whistled.

Modifiers, however, are frequently included in the sentence:

     Adj   S AV V   Adj   S   V — Adv —
    f. A heavy rain is falling.   g. The cold wind blew in the mountains.
        S   V   Adv
    h. That roof leaks badly.

Pattern 2 Subject-Verb-Object (S-V-O) In addition to the subject and verb, Pattern 2 requires a direct object. The verb, as in Pattern 1, is an action verb, and the object may be single or compound.

         S   AV   V   O   S   V   O   O
    a. The waiter has forgotten the water.   b. He served pizza, salad, and
   O   S   S AV   V   O
gelato.   c. Chris and Mike are drinking wine.

Pattern 3 Subject–Linking Verb–Noun Completer (S-LV-NC)   In this pattern, a linking verb connects the subject and the noun completer. The completer may be single or compound.

           S   S   LV   NC   S   AV

a. The Millers and the Burns <u>were</u> neighbors.   b. Ed Burn <u>has</u>

   LV   NC   S   AV   LV   NC

<u>become</u> the governor.   c. They <u>will</u> <u>remain</u> friends.

Pattern 4 Subject–Linking Verb–Adjective Completer (S-LV-AC)   The first three sentence patterns require only nouns and verbs. In this pattern, the verb links an adjective to the subject. The adjective completer may be single or compound.

           S   AV   LV   AC   AC   S   LV

a. The weather <u>has</u> <u>turned</u> warm and sunny.   b. The pitcher <u>looks</u>

   AC   S   LV   AC

confident.   c. That decision <u>seemed</u> fair.

EXERCISE 3.11

Complete the sentences by filling in the appropriate subjects, verbs, direct objects, noun completers, and adjective completers. Identify the sentence patterns on the lines at the right.

Sentence Pattern

Example: Traffic was <u>heavy</u>.   S-LV-AC

1. Our conference was a/an _____ .   _____

2. I have lost the _____ .   _____

3. _____ growl.   _____

4. Troy likes _____ .   _____

5. The child _____ and _____ .   _____

6. That lesson seems _____ .   _____

7. _____ and _____ are dancing.   _____

8. Marie has become a/an _____ .   _____

9. Mr. McBride bought a/an _____ .   _____

10. This T-shirt is _____ , _____ ,   _____

    and _____ .

Expanding the Sentence

4.1 *Adding Details with Adjectives*

The sentences you completed for the exercises in the first three chapters are just a beginning. Readers usually ask more of the writer—more color, more variety, more information—in short, more specific details. Adjectives added to nouns, and adverbs added to verbs give the reader additional information by further describing and qualifying the nouns and verbs.

Adjectives

An **adjective** makes a noun or pronoun specific or concrete by limiting and describing it.

```
        N           N    Adj  Adj  N            Adj        N
a. Zoos protect species. Some new zoos protect endangered species.
        N           N      Adj     N      Adj      Adj
b. Zoos breed animals. Far-sighted zoos breed rare and exotic
    N
   animals.
        N        N    Adj  N        Adj      Adj      N
c. Zoos need support. All zoos need continued public support.
```

© 1994 HarperCollins College Publishers

Kinds of Adjectives

Possessive Pronouns and Possessive Nouns   The possessive form of the pronoun is called an adjective because it describes and qualifies nouns: <u>his</u> book, <u>my</u> book. The possessive form of a noun is also called an adjective. Your reader knows exactly what house you are talking about when you write <u>Gene's</u> house or <u>the Martins'</u> house. The possessive nouns are modifying the noun "house" and are, therefore, adjectives.

EXERCISE 4.1

Bracket all possessive pronouns and possessive nouns.

Example: The bike [riders'] protests were loud when they heard that [their] lanes of traffic would be closed.

1. New York City's chief engineer maintains its highways and bridges.

2. His main job is to keep the city's bridges from decaying and collapsing.

3. Today's larger trucks have ruined many of America's roads and bridges.

4. In addition, although salt is used successfully to melt snow, the salt's acidity has destroyed our highways.

5. The chief engineer's judgments about repairs affect many people's lives.

Noun Markers   Noun markers indicate that a noun will follow.

Noun Markers				
a	that	all	either	more
an	these	any	every	most
the	this	both	few	much
some	those	each	many	neither

Some of these words seem to point to the noun: that truck.

Others limit the noun: _____   few people.

Numbers   All numbers are adjectives. They modify and qualify the noun by telling how many.

Examples: five apples   fifty dollars   twenty-four hours

Descriptive Adjectives   The adjectives above do not actually describe nouns. To give the reader a mental picture of something, the writer chooses adjectives that describe the qualities or characteristics of it.

$$\text{Adj}\qquad\text{N}$$
Six clowns entertained the excited children under the top of the

Adj   Adj   Adj   N
enormous white canvas tent.

              Adj   Adj   N   Adj   Adj   N
A clown with curly orange hair kept falling off a small red tricycle.

Position of Adjectives

1. The adjective usually appears in front of the noun:

Adj   N   Adj   N   Adj   N
spring vacation   freshman class   term paper

2. But the adjective can follow the noun it modifies:

             N   Adj   Adj
The woman's answer was polite but guarded.

These adjectives are completers following the linking verb was.

Adj   N   Adj   Adj
The winning team, laughing and shouting, ran off the field.

These present participles are adjectives modifying the noun team. Notice that two of them, laughing and shouting, follow the noun.

© 1994 HarperCollins College Publishers

Special Forms of Adjectives

1. Sometimes present and past participles are used as adjectives:

    Adj   N   Adj   N   Adj   N   Adj   N

    <u>excited</u> fans   <u>winning</u> pass   <u>opening</u> game   <u>defeated</u> team

2. When a noun precedes another noun, the first noun is used as an adjective to describe or limit the second noun:

    Adj   N   Adj   N   Adj   N   Adj   N

    <u>canvas</u> tent   <u>circus</u> tent   <u>plastic</u> cushions   <u>cotton</u> candy

3. Prepositional phrases are also used as adjectives.

                    N   Adj

    Toshiro sent five letters <u>of application</u>.

<u>Of application</u> specifies the kind of letters that Toshiro sent; therefore, the phrase is an adjective.

EXERCISE 4.2

In the following sentences, bracket all the participles and nouns used as adjectives.

Example: Alex spent an [exciting] time at the [opening pro-football] game.

1. In his box seat, Alex watched a closely fought battle.

2. The turning point came for the home team during the last few minutes of the game.

3. Everyone praised the winning pass of the rookie quarterback and the clever tactics of the head coach.

4. The excited fans roared as the place kicker sent the ball through the uprights of the goal post for the extra point.

5. The winning team, laughing and shouting, ran off the football field.

How to Choose Adjectives

When writers choose adjectives to create a picture for the reader, they are asking themselves questions about their subjects.

1. What kind?

   Example: dancing lessons   "Dancing" tells what kind of lessons.

2. How many?

   Example: ten lessons   "Ten" tells how many lessons.

3. Which one?

   Example: the last lesson   "Last" tells which one.

4. Whose?

   Example: Judy's lesson   Judy's tells whose.

Questions like these can help writers to add details to a sentence.

EXERCISE 4.3

Bracket all the adjectives in the following paragraph.

It is [a] [beautiful], [sunny] day in [a] [popular] [theme] park in [the] United States. Mr. and Mrs. Tomita, on their first trip to this country, listen attentively to a tour guide's claim that thirty-five thousand adults and children visit the park every day. Most visitors to this magical place are attracted by an amazing variety of shows, rides, exhibits, and restaurants. Both Mr. and Mrs. Tomita, however, are impressed by the clean surroundings. They are staying at the vacationland's hotel where all the rooms have immaculately

© 1994 HarperCollins College Publishers

clean blue plastic furniture, green and beige walls, and beds covered with purple-green spreads. The hotel's parking lot, with its carefully planted vegetation, is also sparkling clean. The smallest scrap of litter is sucked underground and rushed via pipes to a fabulous trash compactor. Even the friendly birds do their part by picking some bread crumbs off the restaurant's patio at the hotel. Mr. and Mrs. Tomita know that they will enjoy themselves in this spotless American tourist attraction.

Punctuating Adjectives Before a Noun

Use commas to separate two or more adjectives that modify the same noun if they are not linked by a coordinating connective such as <u>and</u> or <u>but</u>.

Examples: a. The irritated candidate spoke in a lou<u>d</u>, indignant voice.
             b. The reporter's harsh and probing ques<u>ti</u>ons annoyed the candidate. (no comma needed)

EXERCISE 4.4

Insert commas as needed in the following sentences.

1. Bradley and Carol tried to talk to the instructor in the cluttered noisy office he shared with two other people.

2. Twenty-five airline passengers were rescued from the frigid ice-covered Potomac River.

3. Driving a battered rusty old Volkswagen is more fun than driving a luxurious shiny new Cadillac.

4. Walt admired the graceful elegant and stately style of the dancer.

5. Mary insisted on wearing the old-fashioned clumsy worn-out slippers around the house.

Study Chapter 8 for additional material on this use of the comma.

Comparison of Adjectives

Adjectives have three forms: positive (base form), comparative, and superlative. Most adjectives change their form for use in comparisons. For example, **soft, softer, softest** show differences in degree.

Comparative Degree
a. Walt is strong.
b. Dan is stronger than Walt.

The first sentence simply tells us about one quality of Walt: his strength. The second sentence compares Walt's strength to Dan's strength. Stronger is the **comparative** form of the adjective strong.

Superlative Degree
a. Pete is the strongest of all.
b. He the strongest wrestler on the team.

Strongest is the **superlative** form of the adjective strong. Superlative forms are often followed by prepositional phrases as shown in the examples just given.

© 1994 HarperCollins College Publishers

Forming Comparatives and Superlatives

1. Add **-er** to adjectives of one syllable.		Add **-est** to adjectives of one syllable.
Positive	**Comparative**	**Superlative**
rich	richer	richest
sweet	sweeter	sweetest
tall	taller	tallest

Exceptions: good   better   best
               bad   worse   worst

2. Place the words *more* or *most* before adjectives of two or more syllables.

brilliant   more brilliant   most brilliant
dangerous   more dangerous   most dangerous
exciting   more exciting   most exciting

Exception: To form the comparative of two-syllable adjectives ending in **-y,** change the **-y** to **-i** and add **-er.** To form the superlative add **-est.**

happy   happier   happiest
lovely   lovelier   loveliest
lazy   lazier   laziest

Use the comparative form to compare two or more persons, places, ideas, or things.

Use the superlative form to compare more than two persons, places, ideas, or things.

Example: Marion is the tallest player on our team.

Less and Least   Less and least may be substituted for more and most to show a lesser degree in a comparison.

Comparative (followed by *than*)	**Superlative** (followed by *of* or other prepositions)
less dangerous	least dangerous
less comfortable	least comfortable

EXERCISE 4.5

Fill in the blanks with words that show a lesser degree of comparison.

1. The speaker was ＿＿＿＿＿＿＿ interesting than I had expected.

2. Highway 10 is the ＿＿＿＿＿＿＿ dangerous way of all through the mountains.

3. That house is _____ expensive than the one we looked at this morning.

4. I am the _____ creative member of our family.

5. The baby seems _____ sleepy than she was an hour ago.

EXERCISE 4.6

Change the adjective in parentheses into the comparative or superlative degree. The first sentence is completed as an example.

1. Buying a computer for home or business may be the

   <u>most important</u> purchase you will make in the next ten years.
   (important, superlative)

2. The computer you choose for the home will soon be _____
   (easy, comparative)

   to use than the telephone.

3. It will enable you to have a _____ method of controlling the
   (good, comparative)

   family budget.

4. You should be sure to buy a computer that can be upgraded to a

   _____, _____ model sometime in the future.
   (big, comparative) (powerful, comparative)

5. The data-processing computer has become the _____
   (recent, superlative)

   addition to the business world.

© 1994 HarperCollins College Publishers

6. Some computerized information systems offer businesses

    _____ productivity.
    (great, comparative)

7. They even promise _____ use of energy.
                      (efficient, comparative)

8. The use of computers encourages _____ business
                                   (simple, comparative)

   procedures.

9. The _____ computer systems are powerful enough to
       (large, superlative)

   process company payrolls.

10. The computer you buy for home or business should be the

    _____ quality at the _____ price.
    (good, superlative)   (low, superlative)

4.2 Adding Details with Adverbs

Another kind of modifier is an **adverb.** Adverbs add further information about verbs, adjectives, and other adverbs. Study the following tests for an adverb.

Tests for Adverbs

1. Ask the question, When?

   Example: I ran five miles yesterday.
   The word yesterday tells *when* I ran five miles.

2. Ask the question, How?

> **Example:** I ran five miles <u>slowly</u>.
> The word <u>slowly</u> tells *how* I ran five miles.

3. Ask the question, Where?

> **Example:** I ran five miles <u>around the track</u>.
> The words <u>around the track</u> tell *where* I ran five miles.

4. Ask the question, Why?

> **Example:** I ran five miles <u>for my health</u>.
> The words <u>for my health</u> tell *why* I ran five miles.

From these examples, you can see that an adverb can be a single word (*yesterday*) or a phrase (*around the track*). To determine if a word or group of words is an adverb, ask *when, where, how,* or *why*. Adverbs answer these questions.

Function of Adverbs

Adverbs are usually added to a basic sentence to give the reader more information.

Example: She arrived.	basic sentence
She arrived <u>early</u>.	tells <u>when</u> she arrived
She arrived <u>suddenly</u>.	tells <u>how</u> she arrived
She arrived <u>at my door</u>.	tells <u>where</u> she arrived
She arrived <u>to stay with me</u>.	tells <u>why</u> she arrived

Basic Pattern 1 sentences need added information to make them more interesting to your reader. Adverbs add interest and information.

Note: A few words that are usually nouns sometimes function as adverbs.

They tell where he walked:	He walked <u>home</u>.
They tell how far:	He walked a <u>mile</u>.
They tell when:	He walked <u>yesterday</u>.

The adverb tells **the time** the action happened, **the place** it happened, **the manner** in which it happened, and **the purpose** of the action.

Position of Adverbs

The position of an adverb in a sentence is flexible; that is, it can be moved around in a sentence. The position of the adverb <u>occasionally</u> is correct in all the sentences in the following example:

Example: <u>Occasionally</u> she eats in the cafeteria.
She <u>occasionally</u> eats in the cafeteria.
She eats <u>occasionally</u> in the cafeteria.
She eats in the cafeteria <u>occasionally</u>.

EXERCISE 4.7

In the following sentences, write in one-word or prepositional-phrase adverbs of your choice on the lines. The sentences form a paragraph.

Example: Kimiko had been planning her vacation <u>for six months</u>.
(when)

1. Kimiko arrived _____ after a long flight _____ .
(when)   (where)

2. The pilot landed the plane _____ and _____ .
(how)   (how)

3. All the passengers _____ applauded _____ .
(where)   (how)

4. Kimiko walked _____ toward the exit door _____ .
(how)   (why)

5. She was thrilled to be _____ after so many years.
(where)

Comparison of Adverbs

Adverbs, like adjectives, have degrees of comparison: the positive, the comparative, the superlative.

Forming Comparatives and Superlatives

1. To form the comparative of adverbs of *one syllable*, add **-r** or **-er.** To form the superlative, add **-st** or **-est.**

Positive	Comparative	Superlative
late	later	latest
fast	faster	fastest

2. A few adverbs of one syllable are exceptions to rule 1. To form the comparative and superlative of these words, change the spelling of the adverb. Consult your dictionary.

Positive	Comparative	Superlative
far	farther	farthest (physical distance)
far	further	furthest (mental degree)
well	better	best

3. To form the comparative of adverbs of more than one syllable, place <u>more</u> before the adverb. To form the superlative, place <u>most</u> before the adverb.

Positive	Comparative	Superlative
beautifully	more beautifully	most beautifully
carefully	more carefully	most carefully

Exception: badly   worse   worst

Use the comparative form when comparing two actions. Use the superlative form when comparing three or more actions.

Example: I had thought that Jan skated <u>more gracefully</u> than Marie. But then I saw Adele skate after the other two girls. Adele skated <u>most gracefully</u> of all.

EXERCISE 4.8

Change each adverb in parentheses into the comparative or superlative degree. The first is completed as an example.

© 1994 HarperCollins College Publishers

1. Marty Porter, a night school student and the mother of three children under the age of ten, had decided <u>most reluctantly</u> to give
(reluctantly, superlative)
up her full-time job.

2. She found herself performing these three demanding roles

_____ than her own high standards required.
(efficiently, comparative)

3. The inability to organize her activities was not the problem; she

planned each day _____ than the last.
(systematically, comparative)

4. The company she worked for, however, _____
(definitely, superlative)
did not want to lose a valuable employee like Mrs. Porter.

5. Her supervisor arranged a flexible schedule that allowed her to

fulfill _____ her obligations at home, at school,
(easily, comparative)
and at work.

4.3 *Adding Details with Verbal Phrases*

Verbal phrases can be indispensable additions to a basic sentence because they greatly increase the possibilities for expanding it.

Example: Carla waited.

> Breathless and exhausted, Carla waited <u>to hear the choreographer's opinion of her audition.</u>
> <u>Anxious to hear the choreographer's opinion of her dancing,</u> Carla waited, <u>forgetting her exhaustion.</u>

Verbals are formed from verbs and introduce verbal phrases. They usually include a noun and/or a prepositional phrase. They are used as nouns, adjectives, and adverbs in sentences.

1. <u>to choose</u> a pet

The verbal is <u>to choose</u>, formed from <u>to</u> plus the present form of the verb.

2. <u>chosen</u> for its intelligence

The verbal is <u>chosen</u>, the past participle.

3. <u>choosing</u> a Seeing Eye dog

The verbal is <u>choosing</u>, the present participle.

Pay special attention to the first type of verbal phrase (<u>to choose a pet</u>) because it looks like a prepositional phrase. Read the information below carefully.

Note

The word *to* is used to introduce both verbal phrases and prepositional phrases.

TO + A VERB = A VERBAL PHRASE

Example: to travel

TO + A NOUN AND ITS MODIFIERS = A PREPOSITIONAL PHRASE

Example: to the moon

EXERCISE 4.9

A. In the following sentences, bracket all verbal and prepositional phrases.
B. Underline the auxiliary verb once and the main verb twice.
C. Circle the subjects.

Example: Many years ago (Chief Billy Bowlegs) [leading 200 of his Seminole tribe,] <u>hid</u> [in the Florida Everglades.]

© 1994 HarperCollins College Publishers

1. Today 1,500 Seminole Indians live on the reservation built on 120,000 acres of swamp in the Florida Everglades.

2. A group of these Indians, living near Tampa, has defied the law.

3. In addition to a shrine and a museum, the Seminoles have built a drive-thru smoke shop there.

4. The Indians have been selling cigarettes without charging sales tax.

5. From the first, state and local law enforcers did not like these Indians to sell cigarettes.

Punctuation

At the beginning of a sentence, use a comma after an introductory verbal phrase.

Examples: Standing at the end of the line, I had little hope of getting a ticket.
Discouraged by the long line, I gave up and went home.

EXERCISE 4.10

Insert commas after the introductory verbal phrases.

1. Hoping to make a profit Carolyn invested in the stock market.

2. Trying to get to the airport on time Josephine got a ticket for speeding.

3. Snowed in for a week in the mountains we couldn't get back in time to take our final exams.

4. Having spent the day shopping unsuccessfully for shoes Tina decided to wear her old ones to the party.

5. Finding a wallet on his way to school Jerry had visions of a generous reward.

For a more detailed discussion of this use of the comma, see Chapter 8.

4.4 *Misplaced Modifiers and Dangling Modifiers*

When you use modifiers in your sentences, be sure that the word order of each sentence is clear and logical. Placing a modifier in an incorrect position can change or confuse the meaning of the sentence. Modifiers should be placed close to the words that they describe or qualify. Learn to identify and correct **misplaced modifiers** and **dangling modifiers.**

Misplaced Modifiers

Misplaced modifiers are exactly what the term suggests: these modifiers are called misplaced because they have been incorrectly placed next to words that they are not intended to modify.

Examples:

a. I nearly ate all the brownies. (misplaced modifier)

   This sentence suggests that you didn't eat anything at all. You should place nearly in front of *all the brownies.*

   I ate nearly all the brownies. (correctly placed modifier)

b. I heard that our nation needs additional engineers on the television news. (misplaced modifier)

   The engineers are not needed on the television news, are they? You should place on the television news after the verb *heard.*

   I heard on the television news that our nation needs additional engineers. (correctly placed modifier)

c. Coretta bought a German shepherd dog <u>alarmed by the robberies in the neighborhood</u>. (misplaced modifier)

If the dog is alarmed by the robberies, it is not going to make a good watchdog. You should place the verbal phrase modifier in front of *Coretta*.

<u>Alarmed by the robberies in the neighborhood</u>, Coretta bought a German shepherd dog. (correctly placed modifier)

EXERCISE 4.11

Revise the following sentences by placing the words or phrases in parentheses next to the words that they modify.

Example: Eileen ran after the bus. (carrying a heavy briefcase)
<u>Carrying a heavy briefcase, Eileen ran after the bus.</u>

1. Nick saved $100 by making his own repairs on his car. (almost)

_____

2. The candidate promised that he would reduce unemployment.
   (at the political rally)

_____

3. Alfredo ordered a pizza to go.
   (with mushrooms and pepperoni)

_____

4. The painters told us that they would begin painting the house.
   (on Wednesday)

_____

5. Rex saw a woman in the front row jump up and run out the side exit.
   (suddenly)

_____

Dangling Modifiers

A word or a phrase is called a dangling modifier when there is no word in the sentence for it to modify.

Example: Showing an interest in computers, personnel offices are flooded with applications.

Were the personnel offices showing an interest in computers? Of course not. The verbal phrase modifier, Showing an interest in computers, is left dangling. There is no word in the sentence for it to modify. To correct this problem, write the sentence as follows:

Showing an interest in computers, students are flooding personnel offices with applications.

A word such as students must be added to the sentence to eliminate the dangling modifier.

Another method of eliminating dangling modifiers changes the dangling word or phrase into a subordinate clause. You could correct the example given above as follows:

Because students are showing an interest in computers, personnel offices are flooded with applications.

Remember

You cannot get rid of a dangling modifier by moving it around in a sentence. Since there is no word in the sentence for it to modify, you must rewrite the sentence and add the word that the phrase modifies.

EXERCISE 4.12

Rewrite this paragraph on the lines provided. Correct the dangling modifiers in each sentence.

Expecting a robot like R2D2, the robot that was demonstrated to Willy was disappointing. Propelling itself on large wheels, Willy had hoped for useful arms and legs. Having limited mobility, stairs could not be climbed. Responding to voice command, a distance of less than seventy feet was necessary between the robot and its owner. Frustrated by the poor quality, his decision to buy a robot would have to be delayed.

_____

_____

_____

_____

_____

_____

_____

5

Main Clauses

5.1 *Identifying Main Clauses*

When you studied prepositional phrases and verbal phrases, you learned that a phrase is a group of related words without a subject and a verb. A group of related words with a subject and a verb is called a **clause.** There are two kinds of clauses, **main** and **subordinate,** but this chapter will deal only with the main clause (also called an independent clause).

To identify a main clause, look first for the verb and then for the subject. The main clause can stand alone as a sentence if the first word is capitalized and the clause ends with a mark of punctuation such as a period or a question mark. The main clause may also contain words or phrases in addition to the verb and the subject.

EXERCISE 5.1

In the following sentences, identify the underlined group of words as a phrase or a main clause. Write your answer on the line at the right.

1. Many people complain loudly about junk mail.   _____

2. It arrives in large quantities daily.   _____

© 1994 HarperCollins College Publishers

3. <u>Getting on these mailing lists</u> is easy.   _____

4. Companies have always exchanged information <u>regarding consumers.</u>   _____

5. Rented memberships and subscription lists have been another resource <u>used by advertisers.</u>   _____

5.2 *Connecting Main Clauses*

The Simple Sentence

In the preceding chapters, you have been working primarily with the **simple sentence.** The simple sentence contains *one* main clause. Which of the following two sentences is a simple sentence?

1. Mr. Hughes has dreamed of graduating.
2. For a long time since building his first race car nineteen years ago, Mr. Hughes has dreamed of graduating to the NASCAR Grand National Circuit.

Both sentences are simple sentences. Although the second sentence contains several phrases, it has only *one* main clause: one subject and one verb. Both sentences, as you can see, have the same subject and verb:

$$S \qquad AV \qquad V$$

⟨Mr. Hughes⟩ has <u>dreamed</u>

The Compound Sentence

Which of the following two sentences contains *more than one* main clause and, therefore, is *not* a simple sentence?

1. Thousands of drivers like Mr. Hughes test themselves on America's hundreds of small dirt tracks, hoping to win $1,000, $100, or even just a trophy.
2. The race-car drivers hope to make it to the big-league tracks, and they love the thrill of driving at very high speeds.

The first sentence has only one subject and one verb:

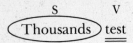

It is a simple sentence with *one* main clause.

The second sentence, containing *two* main clauses, is a **compound sentence.** It has two subjects and two verbs:

$$\text{S} \quad \text{V} \qquad\qquad \text{S} \quad \text{V}$$
(drivers) hope . . . , and (they) love

Now try two more sentences. Which one is a simple sentence: Which one is a compound sentence?

1. Trying to avoid a head-on collision with another car, the driver turned his wheel sharply to the right and crashed into a wall.
2. He wanted to pull off the road, but he could not do it quickly enough.

The first sentence is a simple sentence with one main clause. The clause contains one subject and a compound verb:

$$\text{S} \quad \text{V} \qquad \text{V}$$
(driver) turned and crashed

The second sentence is a compound sentence. It has two main clauses: two subjects and two verbs.

$$\text{S} \quad \text{V} \qquad \text{S} \quad \text{AV} \quad \text{V}$$
(He) wanted but (he) could do

EXERCISE 5.2

A. Begin by circling the subjects and underlining the verbs.
B. Identify each of the following sentences as simple or compound. If the sentence has only one main clause, write S (Simple) on the line at the right. If the sentence has two or more main clauses, write C (Compound) on the line at the right.

Example: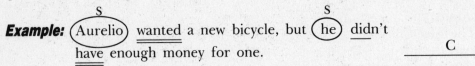

C

1. Some people think of Iowa as flat, but some bicyclists know better now. _____

2. Every year about seven thousand bicyclists ride slowly and painfully across the state of Iowa. _____

3. The ride begins at the Missouri River along the state's western border, and it ends at its eastern edge along the Mississippi. _____

4. Many riders complain about injured knees as well as sunburns. _____

5. The bicyclists are surprised by the hills of Iowa, for the land had looked flat to them. _____

Joining Main Clauses

There are three ways to join the main clauses of compound sentences. You may use (1) a coordinating connective, (2) a semicolon, or (3) an adverbial connective. **Coordinating connectives** (sometimes called coordinating conjunctions) are words used to join words, phrases, or clauses together.

Examples: Karen <u>and</u> Jessica
at work <u>or</u> at school
Karen studies, <u>but</u> Jessica watches TV.

Remember These Seven Coordinating Connectives			
and	for	or	yet
but	nor	so	

Put a comma before the coordinating connective when it joins two main clauses into a compound sentence.

Example: Suzanne was trying to lose weight<u>,</u> so she avoided eating desserts.

EXERCISE 5.3

Change these simple sentences into compound sentences by joining the main clauses with a comma and the coordinating connectives in the parentheses. Circle the subjects and underline the verbs.

1. (but)   The doctor was a well-known specialist. My father would not accept her diagnosis.

2. (and)   The pole vaulter tried again to break the record. This time he succeeded.

3. (so)   It is a large house. They will have room for all their furniture.

4. (for)   Andrea spent four hours a day practicing the flute. She was determined to improve.

5. (or)   We can drive to the beach. We can ride our bicycles.

A **semicolon** (;) may be used to connect main clauses.

Example: Suzanne read the health spa contract several times; she wanted to understand the terms before signing it.

EXERCISE 5.4

Circle the subjects and underline the verbs. On the lines at the right, identify each sentence as simple (S) or compound (C). Correct the compound sentences by joining the main clauses with semicolons.

1. Lucy likes to finish her homework before dinner after eating she gets sleepy.   _____

2. Vivian brought pictures of our high-school class to the reunion everyone laughed at the dated clothes and hairstyles.   _____

3. Arturo and his brother have borrowed money and opened a real estate office. _____

4. Our neighbor was happy about his golf game today for the first time he had a lower score than his wife's. _____

5. The children entertained themselves for half an hour by riding up and down on the escalator. _____

The **adverbial connectives** (sometimes called adverbial conjunctions) listed in the following box also may be used to join main clauses.

Addition:	also further in addition moreover		
Contrast:	however instead nevertheless otherwise		
Time:	meanwhile then		
Result:	as a result consequently thus therefore		
In Reality:	in fact indeed		

Use a semicolon before the connectors and follow them by a comma.

Example: Suzanne has lost ten pounds; <u>therefore</u>, she is proud of herself.

You may need to consult your dictionary to be sure you are using these words correctly.

EXERCISE 5.5

Circle the subjects and underline the verbs. Choose an appropriate adverbial connective from the words in the following box to connect the main clauses in the following sentences. Use each connective only once. Punctuate the sentences correctly.

| consequently | in addition | in fact | instead | then |

1. We had planned to bicycle through England last summer. We painted the house and built a fence.

2. I forgot my umbrella this morning. I was soaked to the skin by the time I reached the office.

3. Milt works six hours a day and overtime on weekends at a restaurant. He takes three classes at a community college.

4. First Norman reads the comics. He settles down to enjoy the sports section.

5. Cindy looked very different with her new haircut. I hardly recognized her.

Punctuation

In simple sentences, some adverbial connectives serve as adverbs and are enclosed by commas. These adverbs do not join main clauses in a sentence as the adverbial connectives do.

Examples: Eric sometimes guesses correctly the meanings of words.
He should, nevertheless, consult a dictionary.

EXERCISE 5.6

Punctuate the following sentences correctly.

Example: A dictionary, indeed, can tell you the meaning of a word.

1. Besides that a dictionary shows you how to spell a word.

2. A dictionary in addition shows you how to divide a word into syllables.

3. It can tell you furthermore the origin and development of a word.

4. A dictionary in fact is a good source of biographical information.

5. You must however develop the habit of consulting it frequently.

5.3 *Parallel Structure*

Coordinating connectives join words, phrases, or clauses that are of equal importance. The word to notice in this definition is equal. Parallel structure, the placing of similar items in similar grammatical form, gives the writer another strategy for expanding a sentence in a balanced way.

Example a: Donna Chapman is a ranger.

Donna Chapman, former gardener, secretary, and short-order cook, is now a ranger in a large national park.

Parallel nouns (gardener, secretary, and short-order cook) give the reader more information about Ms. Chapman.

Example b: She loves her job.

She loves her job giving information to people, keeping the park in order, and preserving the natural beauty of the wild areas.

Parallel verbal phrases (giving ..., keeping ..., preserving ...) add details about the nature of Ms. Chapman's job.

Faulty Parallelism

When you use parallel structure, always put the parts of the sentence that you are joining in the same grammatical form. For example, placing a noun before <u>or</u>, <u>and</u>, or <u>but</u> requires that another noun follow the connective (a swimmer, a golfer, or a jogger). Failure to do so results in **faulty parallelism** (a swimmer, a golfer, or jogging).

Incorrect: Robert liked swimming, dancing, and <u>to play basketball.</u>

Correct: Robert liked <u>swimming, dancing, and playing basketball.</u>

or

Robert liked <u>to swim, to dance, and to play basketball.</u>

EXERCISE 5.7

In the following paragraph, underline all the words, phrases, and clauses that are parallel to each other.

Donna Chapman, former gardener, secretary, and short-order cook, is now a ranger in a large national park. She loves her job giving information to the people, keeping the park in order, and preserving the natural beauty of the wild areas. Every morning she puts on her uniform, packs her lunch, and rides her bicycle to her station, eager to start her work. She especially likes talking to the people who come to vacation in the park. Most faces are new to her, but others are familiar. Some park "regulars" have been coming there for thirty years. Whether it is sunny or rainy, sizzling or freezing, the visitors arrive to enjoy nature and to hike in the woods with their friends and

© 1994 HarperCollins College Publishers

families. Dedicated and enthusiastic, Donna Chapman is at her station, answering questions and being helpful. After shifting from job to job, she has found the one occupation that suits her perfectly.

Punctuation

Use commas to separate three or more items in a series. The items may be single words, phrases, or clauses.

Example: Marty is taking courses in economics, typing, accounting, and statistics this semester.

EXERCISE 5.8

Insert commas where necessary.

1. Jackson Pollock dripped sand pebbles rocks and acrylic paint onto his canvases.

2. The orchestra will travel to Venezuela Argentina Peru Chile and Brazil on a tour of South America.

3. Jo Anne took a bath went back to her room closed the door turned on the radio and lay down on her bed.

4. Rita has never liked to clean to cook to iron or to shop.

5. On weekends Joseph enjoys flying hang gliders going deep-sea fishing or riding horseback.

See Chapter 8 for a more detailed explanation of this use of the comma.

5.4   *Correcting Comma Splices and Fused Sentences*

In 5.2, you learned that main clauses may be joined together with connecting words and appropriate punctuation marks. But sometimes students try to join main clauses without any connecting words or punctuation marks.

      S   V   S   V

1. The (team) won the tournament, (they) received a trophy.

      S   V   S   V

2. The (team) won the tournament (they) received a trophy.

The error in sentence 1 is called a **comma splice** (CS). Sentence 2 is called a **fused sentence** (FS).

    Correct comma splices and fused sentences in any *one* of the following ways:

1. Use a comma and a coordinating connective.

   The team won the tournament, <u>and</u> they received a trophy.

2. Use a semicolon.

   The team won the tournament; they received a trophy.

3. Use an adverbial connective and a semicolon and comma.

   The team won the tournament; <u>therefore</u>, they received a trophy.

4. Use a period and a capital letter.

   The team won the tournament. <u>T</u>hey received a trophy.

EXERCISE 5.9

Circle the subjects and underline the verbs in each sentence. Decide if there are two main clauses. On the line at the right, write CS for comma splice, FS for fused sentence, or NE for no error. Then punctuate the sentences correctly.

1. The children ran around the park their mothers tried to quiet them unsuccessfully.   _____

2. The traffic was unusually heavy this evening, it was caused by an accident at the intersection.   _____

3. The smog disappeared after the heavy rains it reappeared in a few days.   _____

4. In the early morning, many joggers are running.   _____

5. It was late, and all the lights in the house were out.   _____

EXERCISE 5.10

Correct these comma splices and fused sentences by using coordinating connectives, semicolons, or adverbial connectives with correct punctuation.

1. More corporations are beginning to open day-care centers for their employees' children, the centers are open from nine to five.

2. Working parents take fewer days off if their children are well cared for they worry less.

3. Two-paycheck families appreciate the cost benefits, the price of a full-time babysitter would use up an entire salary.

4. Single-parent families especially appreciate the convenience of quality child-care programs child-care programs help to recruit high-quality employees.

5. Government support helps the corporations build special facilities, pre-school playgrounds and indoor classrooms are often too expensive for smaller corporations to construct.

6
Subordinate Clauses

6.1 *Identifying Subordinate Clauses*

A **main clause** is a group of words with a subject and a verb. It is called a simple sentence when the first word is capitalized and it ends with a period, a question mark, or an exclamation point.

Example: (We) enjoy eating ice cream. (main clause or simple sentence)

A **subordinate clause** (or dependent clause) is a group of words with a subject and a verb that is introduced by a subordinator. It is not called a sentence because it makes an incomplete statement.

(subordinator)
Example: because (we) enjoy eating ice cream

The following subordinate clauses are incomplete by themselves. They should not be followed by periods.

Examples:

1. While the band took a break

2. Since you went away

They leave a question unanswered. You want to ask:

1. What happened while the band took a break?
2. What has happened since you went away?

They need another clause, the main clause, to answer these questions. You might complete the sentences as follows:

1. While the band took a break, I soaked my feet.
2. Since you went away, I found another job.

The difference between a main clause and a subordinate clause is often only the *addition* of one word at the beginning of the clause. If you add a subordinator to a main clause, you make a subordinate clause.

Example: He bought a van. (main clause)
            when he bought a van (subordinate clause)

Subordinators (partial list)	
Place:	where, wherever
Time:	after, before, when, whenever, as, since, until, as soon as, while, as long as
Cause or Purpose:	so that, in order that, as, because, since, that, why
Condition:	if, unless, when, whether
Contrast:	although, even though, while
Concession:	as if, though, although
Comparison:	than
Identification:	that, who, what, whom, whose, which

Some of these words function as subordinators in some sentences and as prepositions in other sentences.
    The <u>subordinator</u> is followed by a subject and a verb.

Example: before (I) go to work = subordinate clause

The preposition is followed by a noun and its modifiers.

       Prep   N

Example: before the performance = prepositional phrase

Notice that like is not a subordinator. Therefore, it is incorrect to say, "Like I said, . . ." The word like is only used as a preposition.

   A sentence that has a main clause and one or more subordinate clauses is called a **complex sentence**.

EXERCISE 6.1

In the following complex sentences, underline the subordinate clause and put parentheses around the subordinator. Begin by circling the subjects and underlining the verbs.

Example: (Since) (butter) costs too much money, many (people) use margarine.

1. The guests left after the party was over.

2. The animals performed their tricks although the audience did not applaud.

3. When the instructor passed back our papers, I was delighted.

4. Mr. Hashimoto has been wearing a cast because he broke his leg.

5. While we were riding our bicycles, someone stole our car.

Sentences with More than One Subordinate Clause

1. When the instructor passed back our papers, I discovered that my grade was an "A."

In this sentence, there are two subordinate clauses. Put parentheses around the two subordinators. (You should have marked <u>when</u> and <u>that</u>.)

2. If you want to travel to Europe this summer, you must save all the money that you earned while you were working as a waitress.

In this sentence, there are three subordinate clauses. Put parentheses around the three subordinators. (You should have marked <u>if</u>, <u>that</u>, and <u>while</u>.)

EXERCISE 6.2

In the following complex sentences, underline the subordinate clauses and put parentheses around the subordinators. Begin by circling the subjects and underlining the verbs.

1. After dinner, while the guests sat around the table, many of them told interesting stories about their work as we all listened attentively.

2. Although she said that she loved him, he didn't believe her because he knew that she went out with many other men.

3. As long as you haven't eaten your lunch yet, you might as well wait until dinner time when we will have a big meal.

4. Before I knew what was happening, the red sports car passed my car as I drove up the hill.

5. The judge said that I should go to driving school so that I would learn about the dangers of drunk driving.

6.2 Using Subordinate Clauses

Subordination, the use of subordinate clauses, gives writers another option for adding ideas to their sentences and variety to their writing. In addition, the subordinator shows the precise relationship between the subordinate clause and the main clause of the sentence.

Example:

1. (Mario) was in Rome. A (thief) stole his wallet.
     (main clause)   (main clause)

2. (When) (Mario) was in Rome, a (thief) stole his wallet.
   (subordinate clause)   (main clause)

By using subordination in sentence 2, the writer makes the time and place of the theft exact and emphasizes one idea—the theft of the wallet. Combining these two main clauses into one complex sentence also improves the style.

Most subordinate clauses can be divided into two major groups: adverb clauses and adjective clauses. Some subordinate clauses are used as noun clauses: Mario knew that he had been careless with his money. The subordinate clause is the direct object of the verb "knew."

Adverb Clauses

In adverb clauses, the most frequently used subordinators specify place, time, cause, condition, and contrast when indicating the relationship between main and subordinate clauses:

Place:	where, wherever
Time:	after, before, when, whenever, as, since, until, as soon as, while
Cause:	because, since, as
Condition:	if, whether, unless, whatever, when
Contrast:	although, even though, while, whereas

Adjective Clauses

The **adjective clause** is also called a relative clause because the subordinator "relates" the rest of the subordinate clause to a word or a word group in the main clause. The subordinate clause is an adjective modifying that part of the main clause by adding information about it.

Subordinators
who   whom   whose   which   that

Examples:

1. The (people) on the bus had offered to help him, and (Mario) thanked them. (two main clauses)

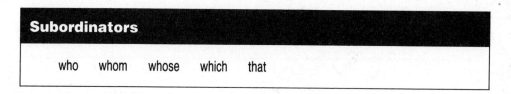

2. (Mario) thanked the (people) on the bus ((who)) had offered to help him. (one main clause and one subordinate clause)

The second sentence improves an awkward sentence by subordinating the first clause in sentence 1 to the second clause. The subordinate clause clarifies the situation by restricting the word people to those who helped Mario.

EXERCISE 6.3

Combine the following sentences into complex sentences.
A. Form a subordinate clause by placing the subordinator in parentheses in the position indicated by the caret (˄).
B. Make any necessary changes in the punctuation and in the capitalization.

Example: ˄ Ty Cobb, nicknamed "The Georgia Peach," was one of the greatest of all baseball players. He was a bitter, angry man. (Use although.)

Although Ty Cobb, nicknamed "The Georgia Peach," was one of the greatest of all baseball players, he was a bitter, angry man.

1. His lifetime batting record ⌃ was 4,191 hits in 24 seasons. It remained unbroken until the summer of 1985. (Use which, omit It.)

_____

_____

_____

2. Cobb ⌃ was a multimillionaire. He gave financial help to young college students, endowed a hospital in his hometown, and gave anonymous aid to indigent ballplayers. (Use who, omit He.)

_____

_____

_____

3. He remained a public idol to many. ⌃ Most of his fans were ignorant of his violent disposition. (Use since.)

_____

_____

_____

4. Cobb welcomed a fight. ⌃ He was sick and old. (Use even when.)

_____

_____

_____

5. Cobb threatened to use a loaded handgun. ⋏ He carried it with him. (Use <u>that</u>, omit <u>it</u>.)

_____

_____

_____

    We often combine ideas by coordinating them—that is, by linking them with the words <u>and</u>, <u>but</u>, <u>or</u>. Coordination works well when the parts are of equal importance, but when the ideas are not of equal importance, it's better to subordinate one idea to another.

Using Subordination to Correct Comma Splices and Fused Sentences

Subordination gives you another way to correct **comma splices** and **fused sentences** by placing one idea in a subordinate clause and the other in a main clause.

Example: My brother joined the merchant marine, he was eighteen. (comma splice)

Correction: My brother joined the merchant marine when he was eighteen.

EXERCISE 6.4

Correct the following comma splices and fused sentences. Join the ideas in the main clauses into a complex sentence by changing one main clause to a subordinate clause. Use the subordinator in the parentheses. Punctuate the sentence correctly.

Example: (since) Ed joined the merchant marine he has been in many foreign ports.

Correction: Since Ed joined the merchant marine, he has been in many foreign ports.

1. (because) The coach was fired his team never won a game.

   _____

2. (when) The cat dug holes in my flower bed, I chased it away.

   _____

3. (although) They lost the first game they won the second one.

   _____

4. (while) We were riding our bicycles, someone stole our car.

   _____

5. (who, omit *she*) Toni is a full-time college student, she works thirty hours a
   week as a musician.

   _____

Punctuation

At the beginning of a sentence, use a comma <u>after</u> a subordinate clause.

Example: <u>When Alex reached the parking lot</u>, he couldn't find his car.

Do not use a comma before a subordinate clause at the end of a sentence.

Example: Alex couldn't find his car <u>when he reached the parking lot</u>.

   Use commas to enclose clauses containing nonessential material. The information may add some details, but the reader could understand the main
idea of the sentence if the clauses were left out.

Example: Stan, <u>who arrived late</u>, had to sit in the last row.

Omit the words enclosed by commas, and the sentence reads:

   Stan had to sit in the last row.

The main idea of the sentence is unchanged.
   Do not use commas to enclose clauses that are essential to the meaning of the sentence.

Example: The people <u>who arrived early</u> had the best seats.

If the subordinate clause is omitted, the main idea of the sentence is lost: The people had the best seats. The clause is needed to identify the people—those who arrived early.

EXERCISE 6.5

Insert commas where necessary. Some sentences do not need commas added.

1. Jeanine's dog which is a poodle digs holes in the backyard.

2. The student who will be the first speaker at graduation was in my history class last semester.

3. The *Queen Mary* which was once an ocean-going luxury liner is docked in Long Beach.

4. Their new stereo which was more expensive than ours has excellent fidelity.

5. The traffic light that is on the corner of Fifth and Grand is not working this morning.

6.3 *Sentence Fragments*

A **sentence fragment** is a group of words that begins with a capital letter and ends with appropriate punctuation such as a period, but the group of words does not express a complete thought or contain a complete main clause.

Some professional writers use fragments in magazines and books. We hear sentence fragments used in conversation, as in the following example:

"Did you leave school early yesterday?"
"Yes, after my music class."

Although the last bit of dialogue begins with a capital letter and ends with a period, it is not a complete sentence. It is a sentence fragment. When used in formal writing, fragments tend to confuse the reader.

Four Types of Sentence Fragments

It will be easier for you to correct fragments in your own writing if you learn to recognize four types of fragments.

Punctuating Subordinate Clauses as Sentences
Identifying the Error: When Jean came home.

This is the most common form of fragment. This subordinate clause is punctuated like a sentence.

Correcting the Error: When Jean came home, she turned on the stereo.

1. You can, of course, simply remove the subordinator, and you will have a complete sentence.
2. More than likely, however, the fragment will appear among the sentences of a paragraph you are writing. Therefore, you should connect the fragment to a sentence that is before or after the subordinate clause and change the punctuation.

(Error) We had just finished dinner. When Jean came home. (frag.)
(Correct) We had just finished dinner when Jean came home.

Note

When a subordinate clause is at the beginning of a sentence, place a comma after it.

Missing Subjects or Missing Verbs

Identifying the Error: 1. Swims for an hour in the pool.
                            2. A place to study with few interruptions.

1. Swims for an hour in the pool. Swims is a verb, but both nouns (hour and pool) are objects of the prepositions for and in. So this is a fragment because there is no subject.
2. A place to study with few interruptions. Place is a noun that could serve as a subject, and although study can be a verb, that is not the case here. In this word group, to study is a verbal. So, again, this is a fragment.

Correcting the Error:

Add a subject and/or a verb to each phrase to make a sentence.

               S

(Correct) Carla swims for an hour in the pool.

               S

(Correct) Ken needed a place to study with few interruptions.

Using Verbals Instead of Verbs or Participles without Auxiliaries

Identifying the Error: Riding our bicycles on the bike path.

In this case, the writer mistakes the verbal for a main verb and also leaves out the subject.

Correcting the Error:

1. Supply an auxiliary verb and, if necessary, a subject.

   (We) were riding our bicycles on the bike path.

2. Attach the fragment to the sentence preceding it or to the one following it.

(verbal phrase)

(We) enjoyed ourselves, riding our bicycles on the bike path.

(verbal phrase)

Riding our bicycles on the bike path, (we) met several friends there.

3. Supply a verb and a completer. The verbal phrase <u>riding our bicycles</u> serves as the subject of thc sentence.

(Riding our bicycles) on the bike path <u>is</u> good exercise.

Using Lists and Examples Not Connected to a Subject and Verb

Identifying the Error: 1. The pattern, pinking shears, straight pins, and the material.

2. For example, my Psychology 1 final last semester.

A fragment is frequently a list or an example explaining some thought that the writer has just expressed. This kind of fragment often begins with one of the following words:

also	first	including
especially	for example	such as
except		

Correcting the Error:

Although you could turn the fragment into a sentence by supplying its own subject and verb (For example, my Psychology 1 final last semester was too long.), generally, you should connect the fragment to the sentence preceding it:

1. First, assemble the items you will need to cut out your skirt: the pattern, pinking shears, straight pins, and the material.
2. Some examinations are not fair, for example, my Psychology 1 final last semester.

© 1994 HarperCollins College Publishers

EXERCISE 6.6

Change the fragments to a sentence in the spaces provided.

1. Michelle has completed almost all the courses required by her major. Except for English 1, Psychology 2, and History 17.

   _____

   _____

2. Shelby has big plans for the sweepstakes money if he wins it. For example, traveling to many foreign countries. Including several in Africa.

   _____

   _____

3. This fabric offers a number of advantages for traveling in the summer. Such as being washable, quick-drying, wrinkle-free, and lightweight.

   _____

   _____

4. She passed the time on jury duty by knitting. And by working crossword puzzles.

   _____

   _____

5. The instructor reviewed the material to be covered in the chapter test. Especially calling our attention to the last three pages.

   _____

   _____

EXERCISE 6.7

Mark F for fragment and S for sentence on the lines at the right.

1. The lifeguard talking to those children is Kim's
   sister.   _____

2. Handle that package with care.   _____

3. The kite twisting and turning before falling to the
   ground.   _____

4. Whenever he does the shopping.   _____

5. And will come home Tuesday.   _____

6. First by cutting down on unnecessary purchases.   _____

7. Turning off the light, José climbed into bed.   _____

8. The job that he wanted.   _____

9. Wondering what she would do until payday.   _____

10. Because I could not find a parking space.   _____

7

Agreement

7.1 *Subjects and Verbs*

Identifying the subject and the verb is the first step in correcting subject-verb agreement errors. The verb agrees in person and number with its subject.

The subject and the verb must agree in number.

A <u>singular</u> subject (one person or thing) takes a <u>singular</u> verb.

> The bird sings.
> The wheel turns.
> The student reads.

A <u>plural</u> subject (more than one person or thing) takes a <u>plural</u> verb.

> The birds sing.
> The wheels turn.
> The students read.

From these examples, or from a review of verb endings in Chapter 2, it should be clear that the singular verb in the present tense ends in **-s.**

A subject and a verb agree if you use the correct form of the verb with the subject. Add an **-s** to the singular verb in the present tense when the subject is he, she, or it, or a singular noun which can be replaced by he, she, or it.

In order to be sure that the verb agrees with the subject, mentally change the noun subject into a pronoun and then select the correct form of the verb.

Examples:

1. Bill walks to work. (Mentally change the subject Bill to he.) He walks to work.

2. Sarah drives a car. (Mentally change the subject Sarah to she.) She drives a car.

3. This pencil needs to be sharpened. (Mentally change the subject pencil to it.) It needs to be sharpened.

4. The tennis players run after the balls. (Mentally change the subject tennis players to they.) They run after the balls.

Again, notice that for singular verb form (the one with he, she, or it) you add an **-s** to the end of the verb in sentences 1, 2, and 3. In sentence 4, **-s** is not added to the verb run because the subject tennis players is plural.

EXERCISE 7.1

Rewrite each of the following sentences, making the subjects and the verbs singular. Some sentences may require the addition of a modifier, such as a or the. Keep all verbs in the present tense.

1. Palm trees give little shade.

   _____

2. The students like the Spanish class.

   _____

3. Old photographs are faded.

_____

4. The bus drivers collect our fares.

_____

5. Her cars require frequent repairs.

_____

7.2   *Subjects and Verbs—Four Difficult Patterns*

Words that Come Between the Subject and the Verb

Words that come between the subject and the verb do *not* change subject-verb agreement.

Examples:

1. The <u>runners</u> on our track team <u>win</u> a trophy every year.

   The subject <u>runners</u> is plural, so the verb <u>win</u> is plural. The words on our track team that come between the subject and the verb do not affect the agreement.

2. The lions, waiting in front of their trainer, obey his commands.

   The subject _____ is plural, so the verb _____ is plural. The words <u>waiting in front of their trainer</u>, that come between the subject and the verb do not affect the agreement. (The subject is <u>lions</u> and the verb is <u>obey</u>.)

3. The jacket that I bought with two pairs of trousers was a bargain.

   The subject _____ is singular, so the verb _____ is singular. The words that I bought with two pairs of trousers do not affect the
   agreement. (The subject is jacket and the verb is was.)

EXERCISE 7.2

Circle the subject and enclose in parentheses any words that come between
the subject and the verb. Then underline the correct form of the verb. The
first sentence serves as an example to follow.

1. Today the (purpose) (of many zoos in large cities) (is, are) not the same
   as in the past.

2. Until this century human visitors to the zoo, not the animals, (was, were)
   the first consideration.

3. An animal in one of these new zoos no longer (spends, spend) its life in a
   cramped cage.

4. Open-range quarters, like those in San Diego's Wild Animal Park, (gives,
   give) these creatures the room to live naturally.

5. Zoo keepers, whenever possible, (works, work) to preserve and protect ex-
   otic species.

Reversed Word Order

A verb agrees with the subject even when the subject comes *after* the verb.

Examples:

1. Waiting for me at home were two hungry (pets.)

   Do not mistakenly identify "home" as the subject. The object of a preposition does not affect the form of the verb. The plural subject pets that
   comes after were requires a plural verb.

The way to find the subject (so you will know how to make the verb agree) is to rearrange the sentence by placing the subject before the verb.

At home were two hungry (pets.)
(becomes)
Two hungry (pets) were at home.

2. There are several (reasons) for his absence.

The plural subject reasons that follows the verb are calls for a plural verb.

3. Here is your (ticket) for the plane trip.

The singular subject ticket that comes after the verb is requires a singular verb.

In general, when sentences begin with there, here, and where, the subject follows the verb. Rearrange the sentence to find the subject:

Here is your (ticket) for the plane trip.
(becomes)
Your (ticket) for the plane trip is here.

EXERCISE 7.3

Circle the subject. Underline the correct form of the verb in each sentence. The first sentence has been completed as an example.

1. There (is, are) (disagreement) on the seriousness of indoor air pollution.

2. Some researchers say that there (is, are) much to be learned about controlling indoor air quality.

3. Experts agree that there (is, are) greater chances of problems developing in older homes.

4. The first clue that a home may have a problem (is, are) often increased humidity.

5. Increased humidity in an insulated home (signals, signal) that the rate of air change is low and other air pollutants may be building up.

Compound Subjects Joined by and

Compound subjects joined by and usually take a plural verb.

```
          S ─────────── S      V
```

Example: Ice cream and yogurt are equally delicious.

The subjects in this sentence are ice cream and yogurt.
They are joined by and, so the verb "are" is plural.

Compound Subjects Joined by or, Neither...nor, or Either ...or

When subjects are joined by these connectives, the verb agrees with the subject *closer* to the verb.

```
          S ──────────── S  ◀── V
```

Example: Neither the instructor nor the students want to work hard today.

The nearer subject, students, is plural, so the verb want is plural.

EXERCISE 7.4

Circle the verb that best completes each sentence.

1. A radio and a cassette player (is, are) included in the price of the car.

2. The radio and the cassette player (was, were) already installed at the factory.

3. Tomatoes and onions (is, are) good in a salami sandwich.

4. Coffee or dessert (is, are) included with the dinner.

5. The lawyer or his secretary (answer, answers) the phone.

EXERCISE 7.5

Circle the subject closer to the verb. Underline the correct form of the verb in each sentence.

1. Either cake or cookies (tastes, taste) good with ice cream.

2. Neither the union members nor the president of the company (seem, seems) willing to compromise.

3. Neither my brother nor my sisters (was, were) college graduates.

4. Either fresh flowers or a bottle of wine (make, makes) a welcome gift.

5. Neither the students nor the instructor (hears, hear) the fire alarm.

EXERCISE 7.6

Insert the form of the verb have that best completes each sentence. Choose either has or have.

1. The telephone and the front doorbell in an apartment _____ not been working

2. The tenants and the landlord _____ tried unsuccessfully to solve the problem.

3. The electrician and the telephone repairperson _____ been trying to make an appointment to fix the bells.

4. Neither the landlord nor the tenants _____ been able to hear the knock on the door.

5. Because the workers cannot get into the apartment, neither the telephone nor the front doorbell _____ been fixed.

7.3   *Subjects and Verbs—Special Problems*

Subjects that Are Singular

When used as subjects, the words below take singular verbs.

any	every	no	some	other words
anybody	everybody	nobody	somebody	each
anyone	everyone	no one	someone	either
anything	everything	nothing	something	neither

Examples: Neither of the children likes squash.
Each of them has set a goal.
Everyone is here.
Somebody was knocking at the door.

Neither, each, everyone, and *somebody* are the subjects of these sentences.

EXERCISE 7.7

Underline the correct form of the verb in the parentheses.

1. No one in my class (works, work) during the summer.

2. Each of us (needs, need) a long vacation.

3. Neither of my two best friends (plans, plan) to look for a job.

4. Everybody in the class (spends, spend) the summer relaxing.

5. Nothing (seems, seem) better than that.

© 1994 HarperCollins College Publishers

Subjects that Can Be Singular or Plural

When used as subjects, these six words can be singular or plural, depending upon the noun or the pronoun to which they refer.

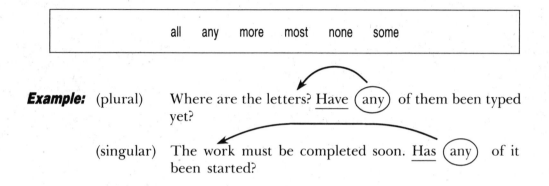

| all | any | more | most | none | some |

Example: (plural)   Where are the letters? Have (any) of them been typed yet?

(singular)   The work must be completed soon. Has (any) of it been started?

Underline the correct form of the verb in parentheses.

1. Karen collects dolls; some (is, are) quite expensive.

2. How many packages did you mail? All of them (has, have) been sent.

3. We prepared the food, but none of it (was, were) eaten.

4. I want a big dish of ice cream. (Is, Are) any left in the carton?

5. We didn't eat the meat because some (was, were) undercooked.

Collective Nouns

Collective nouns represent a collection of persons, places, things, ideas, or activities.

audience	college	crowd	jury	school
band	committee	family	management	society
class	company	government	number	team
		group		

It is often difficult to decide whether a collective noun is singular or plural. Most of the time, use a singular verb or rewrite the sentence to make the subject clearer.

   Instead of saying: "The band are tuning their instruments," you could say, "The band members are tuning their instruments."

Examples:

1. The number of courses offered this semester is small.

2. My favorite musical group is playing at the club all week.

3. Our school band is buying its own bus.

Nouns Ending in -s that Are Not Plural

Physics, economics, mathematics, measles, mumps, and news are considered singular even though they end in **-s,** and they take singular verbs.

Example: (Mathematics) was my favorite subject in high school.

EXERCISE 7.9

Underline the correct verb.

1. Mumps (is, are) a contagious childhood disease.

2. Physics (was, were) a major field of interest for Albert Einstein.

3. Economics (is, are) the most difficult subject in John's schedule.

© 1994 HarperCollins College Publishers

4. The international news (sounds, sound) encouraging for a change.

5. Measles sometimes (cause, causes) meningitis.

Time, Money, and Weight

Words that specify *time, money,* or *weight* require a singular verb when they are considered as a unit even if they are plural in form.

Examples:

1. Two (semesters) is really a short time.

2. Five (dollars) is a modest fee for an entrance exam.

Titles

Titles of songs, plays, movies, novels, or articles require singular verbs even if the titles are plural.

Example: (*The Carpetbaggers*) is both a novel and a movie.

Names of Organizations and Businesses

The names of organizations and businesses that are plural in form but singular in meaning require a singular verb. Substitute a pronoun for the proper noun to determine which verb to use.

                                    S   V

Examples: The Taylor Brothers store advertises in the newspaper every Thursday. (It advertises . . .)

                      —————— S —————— V

The House of Representatives is in session today. (It is in session today.)

Special Problems of Agreement

Who, That, *and* Which *as Subjects* *Who, that,* and *which* used as subjects take singular verbs if the words they refer to are singular. They take plural verbs if the words they refer to are plural.

Examples:

1. (I) know a woman (who) plays the tuba. (The verb *plays* is singular be- cause it agrees with the subject *who. Who* is singular because it refers to *woman,* a singular noun.)

2. (Dogs)(that) bark make me nervous. (The verb *bark* is plural because it agrees with its subject *that. That* is plural because it refers to *dogs,* a plural noun.)

EXERCISE 7.10

Write the noun that <u>who</u>, <u>which</u>, or <u>that</u> refers to on the line at the right. Then underline the correct form of the verb in parentheses.

Example: Businesses that (<u>sell</u>, sells) products for leisure
activities compete with television.   <u>businesses</u>

1. The television set has become a home-entertainment center for Americans who (seeks, seek) recreation during their leisure time.   _____

2. The family of four that usually (goes, go) to a movie theater once or twice a week can now save money, watching cable television at home.   _____

3. People with videotape cassette recorders, which (plugs, plug) into the television set, schedule their favorite programs at hours most convenient for the family.   _____

4. Instead of going to a videogame arcade, many consumers play videogames that (hooks, hook) up to their own televisions.   _____

© 1994 HarperCollins College Publishers

5. And, of course, commercial television, which (has, have) been keeping Americans at home for years, continues to consume one billion hours of their time each day. _____

7.4 *Agreement of Pronoun and Antecedent*

Pronouns are words that refer to nouns, other pronouns, or noun phrases. The **antecedent** (A) is the noun, pronoun, or noun phrase that a **pronoun** (P) refers to.

Example:

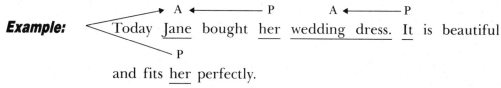

and fits her perfectly.

The first sentence in the example contains a pronoun (her) that refers to the noun antecedent (Jane).

The second sentence contains two pronouns that refer to two noun antecedents in the first sentence.

it (pronoun) = wedding dress (noun antecedent)
her (pronoun) = Jane (noun antecedent)

EXERCISE 7.11

Underline the pronouns and write the antecedents on the line at the right.

                                                                    Antecedent

          A ◄──────── P
Example: Andy hung his diploma on the wall.   ____Andy____

1. At the zoo Tanya and Rosalie fed their peanuts to the monkeys.   _____

2. The engineer completed his report.   _____

3. Have you renewed your driver's license yet?   _____

4. I wondered if the teacher would call on me.   _____

5. John bought two sweaters because they were on sale.   _____

Words that Separate Antecedent and Pronoun

Be sure that the pronoun agrees with the antecedent and not with another noun that may be placed closer to the pronoun than the antecedent is.

                        A   P
1. One of the players injured in the game sprained his ankle.

One is the singular antecedent of the pronoun his, not the plural noun players.

             A ←   A ←   P   P
2. The woman who led the protestors in their march raised her hands in a victory sign.

Her agrees with the singular antecedent woman.

Their agrees with the plural antecedent protestors.

EXERCISE 7.12

Fill in the correct pronoun on the lines in these sentences. Write the word that is the antecedent on the line at the right.

Antecedent

1. The artist who sold me these paintings signed

_____ name in the corner.   _____

2. Some of the visitors left _____ umbrellas here.   _____

3. Mrs. Jones, who owns several apartment buildings, has

won _____ case in court.   _____

© 1994 HarperCollins College Publishers

4. When the birds fly south in the winter, how do

_____ know where to go?   _____

5. Several of the students have completed all of

_____ assignments.   _____

Compound Antecedents

Compound antecedents usually require a plural pronoun.

Example: Betty and Ellie have <u>their</u> own cars.

However, if the two antecedents are joined by <u>or</u>, <u>neither...nor</u>, or <u>either...or</u>, the pronoun agrees with the one closer to the pronoun.

Example: Neither my brother nor my parents would admit that <u>they</u> couldn't solve my sister's algebra problems.

When one subject is plural and the other singular, place the plural subject second to avoid writing an awkward sentence.

Example (awkward)   Did either the plumbers or the electrician estimate how many days he would need to complete the work?

(rewritten)   Did either the electrician or the plumbers estimate how many days <u>they</u> would need to complete the work?

EXERCISE 7.13

Fill in the correct pronoun on the lines in these sentences. Write the word or words that are the antecedents on the line at the right.

Antecedent

1. Both Ralph and George have turned in ＿＿＿＿＿＿ books.   ＿＿＿＿＿＿

2. Mr. & Mrs. Asano have given us ＿＿＿＿＿＿ help.   ＿＿＿＿＿＿

3. Either Martha or Angela will bring ＿＿＿＿＿＿ dictionary to class.   ＿＿＿＿＿＿

4. Did either the gardener or the window cleaners send a bill for ＿＿＿＿＿＿ work?   ＿＿＿＿＿＿

5. Neither Bruce nor Richard pays ＿＿＿＿＿＿ mother any rent.   ＿＿＿＿＿＿

Collective Nouns

The following nouns are usually singular if you refer to the group as a unit:

audience	committee	government	number
band	company	group	school
class	crowd	jury	society
college	family	management	team

                A   P

Example: Our school <u>band</u> bought <u>its</u> own bus.

In this example, you are referring to the band as a unit. If you are unsure whether to use a singular or plural pronoun, rewrite the sentence to make it less awkward.

EXERCISE 7.14

Write <u>its</u> or <u>their</u> on the line in each of the following sentences.

1. The committee made ＿＿＿＿＿＿ recommendation yesterday.

2. The senior class will vote for ＿＿＿＿＿＿ officers tomorrow.

3. Will the jury ever reach ＿＿＿＿＿＿ decision on this case?

4. The audience sat down quietly in ＿＿＿＿＿＿ seats.

5. Last year the company that my father works for gave ＿＿＿＿＿＿ employees a bonus in December.

Singular Words

The words below are singular. Pronouns that refer to these words should also be singular.

any	every	no	some	other words
anybody	everybody	nobody	somebody	each
anyone	everyone	no one	someone	either
anything	everything	nothing	something	neither
				one

      A   P

Example: Has <u>everyone</u> finished <u>his or her</u> test? (not, <u>their</u> test)

The use of <u>their</u> with words like <u>everyone</u> and <u>everybody</u> is gaining acceptance. Many people would agree that it is acceptable to write:

Has everyone finished <u>their</u> test?

When writing assignments for academic purposes, try rewriting the sentence to leave out the pronoun.

Rewrite: Has everyone finished the test?

This solution also avoids the problem of sexist language and the awkward alternative of writing:

Has everyone finished <u>his</u> or <u>her</u> test?

EXERCISE 7.15

Complete the following sentences with appropriate pronouns or rewrite the sentences to avoid problems of awkwardness.

1. Someone left _____ books on that desk.

2. Has anyone brought _____ camera?

3. Each of the girls has paid _____ dues to the club treasurer.

4. Nobody has received _____ grades in the mail yet.

5. Everyone must show _____ employee badge to the guard at the gate.

Note: The repeated use of his/her in a paragraph or an essay can become monotonous or sound forced. You usually can avoid this problem by using a plural noun antecedent and substituting their or by using a noun marker (a, an, or the).

Agreement of Who, Whom, Which, and That with Antecedents

Who, whom, which, and that should agree not only in gender, person, and number with their antecedents, but they should also agree with them in a special way. Who and whom refer only to people.

             A ← P

Correct: 1. Marilyn, who lives next door, wants to be a model.

             A ← P

Incorrect: 2. We have a dog who can shake hands. (Write: . . . dog that. . . .)

Which refers only to animals or to non-human things.

             A ← P

Correct: 1. Roy's car, which is twenty years old, is still running.

© 1994 HarperCollins College Publishers

$$A \longleftarrow P$$

Incorrect: 2. He is a man <u>which</u> anyone would like. (Write: . . . man whom. . . .)

<u>That</u> may refer to animals or things. The usual rule has been not to use <u>that</u> to refer to people. However, the use of the word <u>that</u> to refer to people is gaining wider acceptance, especially in conversation. When you are writing formal English, however, it is a good idea to use <u>who</u> and <u>whom</u> in reference to people.

Correct: 1. The <u>car that</u> I bought six months ago is falling apart.

Correct: 2. The <u>two dogs that</u> belong to my neighbor like to dig.

Informal: 3. He doesn't like <u>people that</u> don't agree with him.

Formal: 4. He has no patience with <u>people who</u> do not share his views.

EXERCISE 7.16

Underline the pronoun that best completes each sentence.

1. The people (who, that) live on my street belong to a neighborhood-watch group.

2. I joined the group (who, that) was formed last year.

3. The neighborhood is watched by the people (who, that) live there.

4. There are signs in the windows of the members' houses (who, that) warn criminals to stay away.

5. I like living in a neighborhood (who, that) is safe.

  If you have difficulty knowing whether to use <u>who</u> or <u>whom</u> to introduce a subordinate clause, study the following explanations.

  Use <u>who</u> to introduce a subordinate clause when it is the subject of the verb in <u>that</u> clause.

Example: Mark did not know <u>who</u> had given the money to Alan.

(<u>Who</u> is the subject of the verb <u>had given</u>.)

Use <u>whom</u> to introduce a subordinate clause when it is the object of a verb or a preposition in that clause.

Example: Mark did now know <u>whom</u> Alan had given the money to.

(<u>Whom</u> is the object of the preposition <u>to</u>.)

EXERCISE 7.17

Choose the correct word to complete the following sentences.

1. Anthony, surrounded by the opponent's linemen, did not know (who, whom) was running down the field.

2. Anthony depended on the signals from the coach to tell him (who, whom) to throw the ball to.

3. The coach, (who, whom) had a clear view of the whole field from the sideline, signaled the numbers of the receiver to Anthony.

4. Anthony just threw the ball with all his might, hoping that it would reach the person for (who, whom) it was intended.

5. The fans in the crowd roared when they saw the receiver, (who, whom) was waiting in the end zone, catch the ball.

7.5   Unclear Pronoun Reference

You will confuse your reader if there are two or more nouns the pronoun can refer to or if there is no antecedent at all for the pronoun. Learn to provide one specific antecedent for each pronoun by studying this section.

© 1994 HarperCollins College Publishers

More than One Possible Antecedent

Example: Pete told Max that <u>he</u> was becoming bald.

There are two possible antecedents. <u>He</u> could refer to either <u>Pete</u> or <u>Max</u>.

Revised: Pete said to Max, "I'm getting bald."
Pete told Max that Max was getting bald.

Example: Carol dropped the glass on the plate and broke <u>it</u>.

The antecedent is not clear. Did the glass break? Or was it the plate?

Revised: When Carol dropped the glass on the plate, the glass broke.
The plate broke when Carol dropped a glass on it.

Example: My sister gave a speech at her graduation ceremony. <u>This</u> pleased my family.

<u>This</u> does not clearly refer to a single noun. Either <u>ceremony</u> or <u>speech</u> could be the noun antecedent.

Revised: The speech that my sister gave at her graduation ceremony pleased my family.

No Specific Antecedent

Example: I liked camp because <u>they</u> were so friendly.

The pronoun <u>they</u> cannot refer to the singular noun <u>camp</u>. Substitute a specific noun for the pronoun <u>they</u>.

Revised: I liked camp because the counselors were so friendly.

Example: Her husband is a football coach, but she thinks <u>it</u> is boring.

It surely cannot refer to <u>husband</u> or <u>football coach</u>. Substitute a specific noun for the pronoun it.

Revised: Her husband is a football coach, but she thinks <u>football</u> is boring.

EXERCISE 7.18

The antecedents of the underlined pronouns in these sentences are unclear.
Give the pronouns specific antecedents or replace the pronouns with nouns.
If necessary, rewrite the sentence.

1. Marla told Tess that <u>she</u> had lost <u>her</u> pen.

_____

2. There are so many automobile accidents because <u>they</u> are so careless.

_____

3. Mr. Bronowski is a great surgeon. <u>This</u> is a rewarding profession.

_____

4. Before taking a test, Roberto studies and gets a good night's sleep, <u>which</u> is important.

_____

5. The graduates marched solemnly down the aisle to receive their diplomas. <u>It</u> was so inspiring.

_____

8

Commas

8.1 *Coordinating Connectives Between Main Clauses; Items in a Series; Introductory Phrases and Clauses*

Many writers are confused about when to use commas. Study and memorize the *ten* rules discussed in this chapter, and you will not be confused about the use of commas.

1. Use a Comma Between Two Main Clauses Connected by a Coordinating Connective

Place a comma before a coordinating connective (and, but, for, or, nor, so, and yet) when it joins two main clauses.

Example: The (outfielder) dropped the fly ball, and the (runner) on third base scored.

Unnecessary Commas   The following sentence does not have a comma before the connective. In this sentence, and connects the two parts of a compound verb, not two main clauses.

Example: The outfielder dropped the ball <u>and</u> committed on error.

EXERCISE 8.1

Insert commas where necessary.

1. Andrew did not want to wear his raincoat to school yesterday nor did he want to carry an umbrella.

2. I have seen that movie star before yet I cannot remember her name.

3. Louis and Gerald tried out for the basketball team and both of them were chosen.

4. Brett and Lula were married on Friday morning but they did not leave for Hawaii until Saturday.

5. Athletes must train hard and watch their diet every day or they will not be able to compete.

EXERCISE 8.2

If the sentence is punctuated correctly, write *Yes* on the line at the right. If the sentence is incorrectly punctuated, write *No* on the line at the right.

1. James will have to repair his car, or take the bus to work.   _____

2. Rita has no patience, for waiting in line.   _____

3. The fire started in the garage, and spread rapidly to the house.   _____

4. Angela sometimes drinks root beer, but prefers cola.   _____

5. Mr. Washington frequently sends letters to the newspaper, but the editor has never printed one.   _____

2. Use Commas to Separate Items in a Series

Use commas to separate *three or more items* in a series. The items may be single words, phrases, or clauses. A comma before the last item is optional if there are exactly three items in the series. In the following examples, you may omit the comma before *and* in sentences 2 and 3 if you wish.

Examples:

1. Marty is taking courses in economics, typing, accounting, and statistics this semester. (words)

2. I went to the bank, did some shopping, and returned home by eleven. (phrases)

3. Leroy cut the grass, Cathy pulled the weeds in the flower beds, and Pat trimmed the hedges. (main clauses)

Unnecessary Commas   No commas are necessary in the following sentence because there are only two items in the series.

Example: Tennis and swimming are her favorite sports.

EXERCISE 8.3

Insert commas where necessary.

1. Last semester Evelyn took four classes at college worked twenty hours a week and sang in the church choir on weekends.

2. My favorite breakfast cereal contains the following ingredients: malt barley oats honey and raisins.

3. He caught the pass ran along the sideline for twenty yards into the end zone but failed to score because he had stepped out of bounds on the two-yard line.

4. The students were told to bring their workbooks dictionaries lined paper and pens to every class meeting.

5. The recipe listed the following ingredients: sugar butter flour cocoa walnuts milk and peanut butter.

EXERCISE 8.4

If the circled comma is necessary, write *Yes* on the line at the right. If the circled comma is unnecessary, write *No* on the line at the right.

1. In high school Jason began to worry about going to college ⊙ choosing a career and finding a high-paying job.   _____

2. The chili we ordered for lunch was hot ⊙ and spicy.   _____

3. Namibia, Botswana, Zimbabwe⊙and Mozambique border South Africa on the east, north and west.   _____

4. Dean's favorite authors used to be Ray Bradbury ⊙ and Robert Heinlein.   _____

5. We have expanded our network to include Wisconsin ⊙ Indiana, and Connecticut.   _____

3. Use a Comma After Introductory Words and Phrases

At the beginning of a sentence, use a comma after a long phrase.

Examples:

1. *By the end of the second week of school,* Ken was counting the weeks until Thanksgiving weekend.

2. *Taking out his new camera,* Ken remembered that he had forgotten to buy film.

© 1994 HarperCollins College Publishers

The comma after a single introductory word or an introductory short phrase is *optional*. Although many writers use the comma after these expressions, others do not.

Examples:

1. We waited for forty minutes in the rain for the bus.
   Finally, it arrived, but every seat was taken.

2. When I come home from work every evening, I eat dinner, take a shower, and do my homework. *Last of all,* I eat a snack and watch a television program before I go to bed.

3. *After work* four of us went bowling.

4. *In that heat* no one could sleep comfortably.

If there is any question about the meaning of the sentence, use a comma after a single word or a short phrase of introduction.

> Inside, the theater was cool and dark.
> While riding, the men had difficulty staying awake.

Try reading these two sentences without commas, and you will see why the comma in each case is essential to understanding the meaning.

EXERCISE 8.5

Insert commas where necessary. Some sentences do not need commas added.

1. Within two or three months the parking lot will be less crowded.

2. After a short pause the speaker answered the questions from the audience.

3. Best of all the food is always served hot.

4. In many tropical countries the natives take a siesta in the middle of the day.

5. John has been commuting twenty-five miles a day to school. Fortunately he found an apartment for rent near the college yesterday.

EXERCISE 8.6

If the sentence is punctuated correctly, write *Yes* on the line at the right. If the sentence is incorrectly punctuated, write *No* on the line at the right.

1. During the emergency the water was turned off for six hours. _____

2. While working at the doughnut shop Kathy lost ten pounds. _____

3. Despite many years of lecturing, writing, composing, and performing, the noted pianist had no intention of retiring. _____

4. Jan spent almost an hour shopping for groceries today. Of course, she forgot to buy the one item she needed most. _____

5. Before making the long drive to Seattle we bought two new tires for the car. _____

4. Use a Comma After Introductory Subordinate Clauses

Use a comma after a subordinate clause at the beginning of a sentence.

Example: *When you move to your new office,* send us your address.

Unnecessary Commas Do *not* use a comma before a subordinate clause at the end of a sentence.

Examples:

1. Jay sold his old typewriter _when he bought a new one._

2. Sue had to go to the market _because she forgot to buy milk._

EXERCISE 8.7

Insert commas where they are needed. Some sentences do not need commas added.

1. Although Jo Ellen had always known the truth about Harry she still loved him.

2. Before you can understand calculus you must understand algebra and trigonometry.

3. If the rain doesn't stop soon the rivers will overflow their banks.

4. By the time you are ready to take the test you will be able to answer all of the questions correctly.

5. The thick salmon steak was delicious even though it was a little overcooked.

EXERCISE 8.8

If the sentence is punctuated correctly, write _Yes_ on the line at the right. If the sentence is incorrectly punctuated, write _No_ on the line.

1. Wendell is moving, because the landlord raised the rent. _____

2. After breakfast Victor and Frances drove to a nearby resort where they purchased ski-lift tickets. _____

3. If you need a dictionary and a notebook for class, you
   can buy them at the student bookstore.   _____

4. Nancy is a person, who enjoys giving parties.   _____

5. Richard decided to quit smoking as soon as the
   Christmas holidays were over.   _____

8.2   Adjectives Before a Noun; Words that Interrupt; Direct Address

5. Use Commas to Separate Adjectives Before a Noun

Use commas to separate two or more adjectives that modify the same noun if
they are not linked by a coordinating connective. You can use two tests to tell
whether or not to put a comma between modifiers before a noun.

1. Use a comma if and can be used to connect the adjectives.
2. Use a comma if you can reverse the order of the adjectives.

Example: Bob was the most aggressive, skillful player on the court.

Use a comma because you could say:

1. Bob was the most aggressive and skillful player on the court.
                                    or
2. Bob was the most skillful, aggressive player on the court.

Unnecessary Commas   Do *not* put a comma between adjectives if and cannot be placed between them or if you cannot reverse their order.

Example: He was the most aggressive, skillful basketball player on the
            court.

1. You would not write skillful and basketball player.
2. You cannot reverse the words—basketball skillful player.

© 1994 HarperCollins College Publishers

Therefore, do not put a comma between <u>skillful</u> and <u>basketball</u>.

The adjectives placed before <u>basketball player</u> modify both words. Do not put a comma between the final modifier and the noun.

EXERCISE 8.9

Insert commas as needed in the following sentences.

1. The raindrops fell into the clear blue deep water of the pool.

2. Shana left her discarded smelly clothes scattered around her large sunlit bedroom.

3. The acrobat entertained the huge enthusiastic audience by his skillful graceful performance.

4. In the early morning the joggers run effortlessly along the deserted shell-strewn beach.

5. Marge's pink sunburnt skin looked painful to me.

EXERCISE 8.10

If the sentence is punctuated correctly, write *Yes* on the line at the right. If the sentence is incorrectly punctuated, write *No* on the line.

1. The young woman had a round tanned pleasant face.   _____

2. Calvin found it especially hard to get up on cold, rainy, Monday mornings.   _____

3. Mrs. Vasquez bought four ripe, Bartlett pears for dessert.   _____

4. We spent several hours in the noisy, crowded
   amusement park.   _____

5. Hank bought a yellow stocking cap to wear with his
   green, nylon, ski, parka.   _____

6. Use Commas to Enclose Words that Interrupt

Use commas on *both* sides of a word (or a group of words) that interrupts the
flow of thought in a sentence.

Examples:

1. Airline pilots, <u>by the way</u>, are often cautious automobile drivers.

2. The guests, <u>it seems</u>, are enjoying the party.

3. Several changes in the enrollment procedure, <u>however</u>, are planned for
   the coming semester.

Do not use just one comma; enclose the interrupting word or words between
two commas.

Unnecessary Commas   Do not use commas to enclose prepositional phrases
that do not interrupt the flow of thought in a sentence.

Examples:

1. A car <u>with a flat tire</u> was parked near the exit ramp of the freeway.

2. The dwarf lemon tree grew rapidly and <u>in no time at all</u> produced fruit.

3. Lunch was served immediately <u>after the meeting</u>.

These sentences do not require any commas.

EXERCISE 8.11

Insert commas where necessary.

1. We hope therefore that you will send our refund soon.

2. Karen's parents as a rule drive her to school every day.

3. The jury as a result took four days to arrive at the verdict.

4. The kitchen in fact has not been cleaned since last week.

5. My opinion in the long run is based on the facts as I understand them.

EXERCISE 8.12

If the sentence is punctuated correctly, write *Yes* on the line at the right. If the sentence is incorrectly punctuated, write *No* on the line.

1. Many of our present tax laws, you must admit, should be changed.   _____

2. Jerome has been living in Des Moines, with his parents for nineteen years.   _____

3. There are after all, other ways of dealing with the disposal problem.   _____

4. Burt jumped out of the chair and, in his excitement knocked over his cup of coffee.   _____

5. An exercise program, for example could include a thirty-minute walk after dinner.   _____

7. Use Commas to Set Off Words in Direct Address

Use commas to set off the names and titles of people spoken to directly.

Examples:

1. "Pat, will you please call Dr. Hodge for me?" Paul said.

2. "I called you, Dr. Hodge, to ask for some information," said Pat.

3. "How often should Paul take the medicine, Doctor?" asked Pat.

These three examples show words in direct address at the beginning, in the middle, and at the end of sentences. Notice the use of commas.

EXERCISE 8.13

Insert commas where necessary.

1. I don't entirely agree Jim with your position.

2. Play it again Sam.

3. Ladies and gentlemen of the jury you have heard the evidence.

4. Ella tell me that you love me.

5. I hope Paulette that you will practice your lesson.

EXERCISE 8.14

If the sentence is punctuated correctly, write *Yes* on the line at the right. If the sentence is incorrectly punctuated, write *No* on the line.

1. A vote for me my fellow Americans is a vote for good government.   _____

© 1994 HarperCollins College Publishers

2. Paul, do you have a job for the summer?   _____

3. It is a pleasure to award first prize to you Mrs. Odim.   _____

4. Your suggestion, sir is the best one we have received.   _____

5. We were delighted, Marvelle, to hear about your promotion.   _____

8.3 *Nonessential Words, Phrases, and Clauses; Direct Quotations; Dates, Geographical Names, and Addresses*

8. Use Commas to Set Off Nonessential Words, Phrases, and Clauses

Use commas to enclose words, phrases, and clauses containing nonessential material. The information in these words may add some details, but the reader could understand the main idea of the sentence if they were left out.

Examples:

1. Marcie Evan, who is our pitcher, will be a sportscaster next fall.

2. *Cannery Row,* a novel by John Steinbeck, has been made into a movie.

Omit the words enclosed by commas, and the sentences above read:

1. Marcie Evan will be a sportscaster next fall.
2. *Cannery Row* has been made into a movie.

As you can see, the main ideas of both sentences are unchanged by omitting the nonessential words. In general, if the name or title is given first, the noun appositive or adjective clause that follows is placed within commas.

Unnecessary Commas   Do not use commas to enclose words, phrases, and clauses that are essential to the meaning of the sentence.

Example: Will the person <u>who parked in the loading zone</u> move his car?

If the subordinate clause <u>who parked in the loading zone</u> is omitted, the main idea of the sentence is lost. You are left with *Will the person move his car?* In fact, the person cannot be identified; you do not know who should move his car.

Example: The novel *Cannery Row* has been made into a movie.

In this sentence the title is necessary to identify the book. Therefore, you do not use commas.

In the two examples given, you would *not* enclose the underlined words by commas because they contain material essential to the meaning of the sentences.

EXERCISE 8.15

Insert commas where necessary.

1. My friend Carla Caraway went to New York to get a job as a dancer.

2. A young woman alone in a strange city must learn how to take care of herself.

3. She auditioned for Judith Jamison the famous choreographer of the Alvin Ailey company.

4. Carla breathless and exhausted waited after the audition to hear the choreographer's opinion.

5. Carla joined the Ailey company one of the best dance companies in the world.

EXERCISE 8.16

If the sentence is punctuated correctly, write *Yes* on the line at the right. If the sentence is incorrectly punctuated, write *No* on the line.

1. Dr. Eleanor Fisher, a professor of biochemistry, will be a guest speaker on campus Tuesday noon.   _____

2. Mike unable to remember the answer, skipped the second question and went on to the third.   _____

3. The man jogging around the track was listening to a transistor radio.   _____

4. Farm Fresh the supermarket chain that advertises on TV stays open until 1 A.M.   _____

5. Itzhak Perlman, a renowned violinist performed with the New York Philharmonic last night.   _____

EXERCISE 8.17

Insert commas where required to set off nonessential words, phrases, and clauses.

1. A talented American contralto Marian Anderson who had sung at the White House was barred from singing in Constitution Hall in Washington.

2. Instead Ms. Anderson sang at the Lincoln Memorial before 75,000 people who had gathered in support of her.

3. Three Aaron Copland ballets drawing upon American themes are *Billy the Kid, Rodeo,* and *Appalachian Spring.*

4. Copland wrote *Appalachian Spring* for Martha Graham choreographer and dancer.

5. Ernest Hemingway an American author began his first job as a newspaper reporter at the age of eighteen.

9. Use Commas to Set Off Direct Quotations

Use commas to set off direct quotations from the rest of the sentence.

Examples:

1. "Perhaps," my brother said to me, "you should study once in a while."

2. She asked, "Won't anybody help me?"

3. "I don't want to watch television tonight," Jan said.

4. "I'll be back in an hour," Jim answered, "so don't leave without me."

In sentence 3, although "I don't want to watch television tonight," is a main clause, do not use a period until the end of the complete statement.

Note that commas are placed <u>inside</u> the quotation marks.

EXERCISE 8.18

Insert commas where necessary.

1. "I can never do these homework assignments" Gary complained.

2. "Well" said his mother "you haven't even tried."

3. "I never learn anything in that class" he said "so what's the point?"

4. "Besides" he said to her "I have a date tonight."

5. "Gary, you should do your assignment before you go out" his mother advised.

10. Use Commas in Dates, Geographical Names, and Addresses

Use commas after every item in dates, geographical names, and addresses as shown in the following examples:

Dates: Maria drove to school on Saturday, September 5, 1989.

Geographical names: Miami, Florida, is the site of the Orange Bowl.

Addresses: James's address is 2208 N. McKnight Road, Philadelphia, Pennsylvania 19103. (The zip code is not separated by a comma from the name of the state.)

Unnecessary Commas   Commas may be omitted when the day of the month is not given or when the day of the month precedes the month.

Examples: Maria drove to school in September 1989.
Maria drove to school on Saturday, 5 September 1989.

EXERCISE 8.19

Insert commas where necessary.

1. George will move to Las Vegas Nevada in January.

2. His address has been The Stanford Arms Hotel Apt. 10 536 W. 18th Street Rittman Indiana 46206 for the last six years.

3. We will forward his mail to his new address: The Pyramid Hotel Las Vegas Nevada 89501.

4. The Battle of Gettysburg was fought on July 4 1863.

5. The annual rodeo in Palmdale California features a bull-riding contest.

EXERCISE 8.20

If the sentence is punctuated correctly, write *Yes* on the line at the right. If the sentence is incorrectly punctuated, write *No* on the line.

1. Send Lynn's mail in care of Mrs. R. B. Singer, 1532 Stone Canyon Drive Santa Maria Arizona 85321 starting Friday July 28, 1991.   _____

2. Alfred Holmes was born on February 12, 1950, in Englewood, New Jersey, according to the records.   _____

3. Circle March 15 on your calendar as an important day.   _____

4. Sean and Kathleen left Sunday July 16 for Ireland.   _____

5. Return this form to the Department of Motor Vehicles, 128 S. Cadillac Ave., Newbury, Montana 59711, by Monday, July 3, 1991, to avoid paying a penalty.   _____

9

Punctuation and Capitalization

When you speak, you use pauses, gestures, and changes in the pitch of your voice to signal the beginnings and endings of units of thought. When you read, marks of punctuation provided by the writer guide your understanding of the writer's ideas. When you write, you also must provide guideposts for your readers to help them understand what you mean.

9.1 *Period, Question Mark, and Exclamation Point*

Period (.)

1. Use a period at the end of a sentence to separate it from the next one.

Example: We made plans for a European trip. We studied maps and travel books.

2. Use a period after an abbreviation.

Examples: Mr. Jones   etc.
              Prof. Anderson   P.M.
              Dr. Brown   B.A.

3. Use a period after initials.

Examples: K. C. Jones   Howard C. Smith

4. It is not necessary to use a period in abbreviations that are composed of the first letter of two or more words.

Examples: UCLA   NAACP
              USA   NASA
              CIA   FBI

Question Mark (?)

Use a question mark at the end of a <u>direct question</u>.

Example: Do you really want to go to Europe?

Do not use a question mark after an <u>indirect question</u>, a sentence in which the question is part of the statement.

Example: We asked ourselves if we really wanted to go to Europe.

Exclamation Point (!)

Use an exclamation point after words, phrases, or clauses that express shock or excitement.

Examples: I'm falling!   Help!

Do not overuse the exclamation point. Save it for genuine expressions of emotion.

EXERCISE 9.1

Add periods, question marks, or exclamation points to the following sentences.

1. When did you last study punctuation

2. Mr Newman is a famous actor

3. Help Fire

4. I would be living in New York if I could afford an apartment on E 68th Street

5. He earned his B A degree from N Y U

6. Hal wondered what was wrong with him

7. What is wrong with Hal

8. Hooray We've won the game

9. When we were young, we never questioned why we were poor

10. How are you today

9.2 Semicolon and Colon

Semicolon (;)

1. The semicolon is used as a connector.

A. The semicolon joins two main clauses with closely related ideas to form a compound sentence.

Example: Please give me your history assignment; I was absent from class
yesterday.

B. The semicolon is used before adverbial connectives like <u>however</u>, <u>never-</u>
<u>theless</u>, <u>consequently</u>, <u>therefore</u>, and <u>then</u> to join two main clauses.

Example: The crew was cold and hungry; <u>nevertheless</u>, they worked until
dark.

2. The semicolon is used as a separator. The semicolon is used between
   words or word groups in a series if the items in the series contain one or
   more commas.

Example: Other points of interest in Europe were the Louvre, Paris; the
Colosseum, Rome; and the British Museum, London.

Colon (:)

1. The colon is used at the end of a main clause to introduce a list.

Example: We have always wanted to visit four other countries: Poland, Hun-
gary, Austria, and Switzerland.

2. The colon often comes after words like <u>the following</u> or <u>as follows</u>.

Example: In Austria we would visit <u>the following</u> cities: Vienna, Salzburg,
and Innsbruck.

No colon is used between a verb and the objects or completers that follow it.

Examples: a. The tour (bus) <u>carries</u> the passengers, their guide, and
their luggage.

b. The three (runners) (who) <u>represented</u> our college at the
track meet <u>were</u> Ron Washington, Glenda Thomas, and
Jorge Sandoval.

© 1994 HarperCollins College Publishers

A colon after the verb <u>carries</u> would separate the verb from its objects, and a colon after the verb <u>were</u> would separate the verb from its completers. Remember that a complete sentence must come before the colon.

3. The colon is used after a salutation in a business letter.

Example: Dear Mr. Wilkins:
Please consider me for the position of junior accountant in your firm.

4. The colon separates the hours and minutes when you are writing the time.

Example: Our class meets daily at 10:30 A.M.

Do not use a colon if no minutes are given.

Example: Our class meets daily at 10 A.M.

EXERCISE 9.2

Insert semicolons or colons where needed in the following sentences.

1. The telephone call brought David the news he had been waiting for he had been offered a job in Dallas.

2. First, Brett turned on the television then he poured himself a drink.

3. When baking a carrot cake, one should prepare the following ingredients flour, baking soda, oil, eggs, and carrots.

4. Terri has owned three cars an '80 Buick, an '84 Chevy, and an '88 Ford.

5. Three women who won prizes at the California State Fair were Alice Mills, Sacramento Betty Ford, Palm Springs and Jane Kelly, Modesto.

6. The students had planned to study in the law library however, it was closed when they arrived.

7. The charter flight was scheduled to leave at 3 45 P.M. nevertheless, at 4 P.M. the tourists were still checking in their baggage.

8. The menu lists the following entrees lasagna, fettuccini, and ravioli.

9. It has not rained much this winter therefore, we may have a shortage of water.

10. Come to our house after the movie we will have coffee in the comfort of our home.

9.3   *Quotation Marks*

Direct Quotations

Quotation marks are used primarily in direct quotations. Put quotation marks around the exact words of the speaker.

Examples:

1. Jimmy called, "Anyone for tennis?"

2. "I would rather play golf," replied Lee.

Note the punctuation for direct quotations:

Use a comma before the direct quotation.
Use quotation marks around the speaker's exact words.
Use a capital letter for the first word of the direct quotation.

Split Quotations

Examples:

1. "But, Linda," he said, "you and Cheryl have never ridden on the Colossus."

2. "You go ahead and ride on it," she answered. "We'll stay here and watch you."

Note the punctuation for split quotations:

In 1, the word you begins with a small letter because the words on either side of he said are the two parts of a single sentence.
In 2, there are two sentences. The first one begins with You and ends with she answered. Therefore, the W of We'll is capitalized as the first word of the second sentence.

End Punctuation in Quotations

Periods and commas are always placed inside quotation marks.

Examples:

1. "I would rather play golf," replied Lee.

2. "We'll stay here and watch you."

Question marks and exclamation points are placed outside quotation marks except when the quotation itself is a question or an exclamation.

Example: Did Jimmy say, "I want to play tennis"?

Exceptions:

1. Jimmy called, "Anyone for tennis?" (The quotation is a question.)

2. The crowd shouted, "Touchdown! Touchdown!" (The quotation is an exclamation.)

Quotations within Quotations

Single quotation marks are used to enclose quoted material within a direct quotation.

Example: He never tires of saying, "Remember Patrick Henry's words: 'Give me liberty or give me death.'"

Unnecessary Quotation Marks Do not enclose an indirect quotation in quotation marks. It is a report in different words of what a speaker or writer said. The word "that" usually indicates the following words are an indirect quotation.

Examples:

1. Joan said, "This assignment is Greek to me!" (direct quotation)
Joan said that the assignment was Greek to her. (Indirect quotation, do *not* use quotation marks.)

2. Marcus swore, "I'll never eat at Joe's Pizza Palace again." (direct quotation)
Marcus swore that he would never eat at Joe's Pizza Palace again. (Indirect quotation, do *not* use quotation marks.)

The Use of Quotation Marks and Underlining in Titles

A. Use quotation marks for short works.

1. title of article
2. title of chapter
3. title of short story
4. title of song
5. title of poem

B. In handwritten or typed work, underline the words that would be italicized in printed material.

1. title of book
2. title of magazine
3. title of newspaper
4. title of play, movie, work of art
5. title of record album, compact disc, or video
6. foreign words
7. words used as words

C. Never use quotation marks around the title of your own composition.

Examples:

1. Have you read the article "Getting the Airmail off the Ground" in the May issue of <u>Smithsonian</u>?

2. We decided to rent <u>Gone with the Wind</u> and <u>Fantasia</u> to watch at home.

3. The English instructor assigned two stories for us to read: "A Perfect Day for Bananafish" and "Uncle Wiggily in Connecticut" in the paperback <u>Nine Stories</u> by J. D. Salinger.

4. I bought two CDs at the record store: <u>Maiden Voyage</u> by Herbie Hancock and <u>Miles Ahead</u> by Miles Davis.

5. "Guiding Children's Book Selection," a chapter in <u>Children & Books</u>, contains standards for evaluating books.

6. The word <u>freedom</u> is difficult to define.

EXERCISE 9.3

Use quotation marks or underline as needed in the following sentences.

1. Few people who have read Shirley Jackson's The Lottery or William Faulkner's A Rose for Emily can forget those short stories.

2. Have you seen The Tempest at the Old Globe Theater yet? he asked.

3. Ben said that he had just returned the book Beloved, by Toni Morrison, to the library.

4. The manager ran out of the store and shouted, Stop that shoplifter!

5. Can you believe that Mr. Marquez said, Read the next four chapters by tomorrow?

6. The article A Private Solution to a Public Problem in this morning's Times offers one more proposal to ease the state's financial crisis.

7. When Rose was three years old, her favorite poem was The Owl and the Pussycat.

8. Cheers, Roseanne, and L.A. Law are three television shows that Ron always watches.

9. Poetry and advertising have much in common, according to a chapter entitled Poetry and Advertising in the book, Language in Thought and Action.

10. Lauren obtained material for her speech from the article, College Tuition, in The Atlantic magazine.

9.4 *Hyphen and Dash*

Hyphen (-)

1. Use a hyphen to join two or more words that serve as a single adjective describing a noun.

Example: My son and I had a heart-to-heart talk.

2. Use a hyphen to divide a word at the end of a line of writing or typing. If you are unsure about the correct syllable division, consult a dictionary.

Example: Hazel and Hugh discussed their son's problems together.

Never divide a word of one syllable at the end of a line. Whenever possible, avoid dividing a word.

3. Use a hyphen with fractions, compound nouns, and compound numbers.

Examples: thirty-five   forty-ninth   father-in-law
self-improvement   one-half

EXERCISE 9.4

Insert hyphens where they are needed in the following sentences.

1. A fifty year old man has won the marathon race.

2. Unfamiliar with the city, Steven made a left hand turn into a one way street.

3. I have all my wool sweaters dry cleaned.

4. The sharp eyed detective noticed the run down heels of the suspect.

5. My sister in law Renata bought a second hand typewriter for seventy two dollars.

6. Margot works as a free lance writer; she edits self help books.

7. Two thirds of the Senate voted for the proposed insurance bill covering high risk drivers.

8. The snipers were hiding in the bullet scarred high rise building.

9. As the mayor elect, Mr. Barr was called on to lecture the upper class students of the high school on self reliance.

10. Dennis half heartedly tried self hypnosis to stop smoking.

Dash (—)

A dash signals an interruption in the sentence. Use dashes before and after interrupters.

Examples:

1. Some—but not all—of the problems were difficult.

2. I had volunteered to work this summer—but why bother about that now?

Note: On a typewriter, strike the hyphen key twice to form the dash. Do not overuse the dash. It should not be used as a substitute for commas, semicolons, or colons just because you are unsure about which to use.

9.5 *Capital Letters*

Always Capitalize:

1.	The first word of a sentence and the first word of a line of poetry.	**H**e ran down the street.
2.	The first word of a direct quotation.	He said, "**T**he restaurant is on fire!"
3.	The name of a person.	**A**lbert **E**instein
4.	The personal pronoun *I*.	**I, I**'m
5.	The names of continents, countries, nationalities, states, cities, bodies of water, places, and streets.	**A**sia, **G**reece, **A**merican, **C**alifornia, **D**allas, **P**acific **O**cean, **G**riffith **P**ark, **M**ain **S**treet
6.	The names of the days of the week, months, holidays (but not the seasons).	**S**unday, **M**ay, **M**other's **D**ay, **L**abor **D**ay
7.	The names of commercial products (but not the type of product).	**D**entyne gum, **P**illsbury flour, **I**vory soap
8.	The names of companies, organizations, government agencies and offices.	**G**eneral **M**otors **C**o., **D**emocratic **P**arty, **D**epartment of **M**otor **V**ehicles, **F**ederal **B**ureau of **I**nvestigation

© 1994 HarperCollins College Publishers

9. The titles of persons, books, magazines, newspapers, articles, stories, poems, films, television shows, songs, papers that you write.
Note: Do not capitalize small words like *the, in,* or *a* within titles.

Mr., Dr., Reverend, President Lincoln, "Dream Deferred," *The Jeffersons*

10. The names of schools, colleges, and universities, academic departments, degrees, and specific courses.

West Los Angeles College, Department of English, Associate of Arts, History 101

EXERCISE 9.5

Capitalize where necessary.

1. anh nguyen has become an american citizen.

2. i'm passing english 1, but i'm failing history 21.

3. when mary went to new york, she visited the metropolitan museum of art.

4. i have already seen the play, *phantom of the opera.*

5. sue's favorite lunch consists of ritz crackers, kraft cheese, and coca-cola.

6. when darlene went to sears, she bought wamsutta sheets for her new water bed.

7. are you going to watch the sugar bowl game on new year's day?

8. in the spring i usually spend saturdays working in my garden.

9. yellowstone national park is the largest national park in the united states.

10. my instructor told me to read a novel by hemingway this weekend, but i watched television.

10
Usage

Words that sound alike or look alike can cause many problems in spelling. Study the following words and refer to these pages when you are writing your paragraphs.

10.1   *A / An / And*

1. Use a before words beginning with consonants or consonant sounds.

Examples: a chair, a boy, a tree, a picture, a youth

2. Use an before words beginning with vowels (*a, e, i, o u*) or a silent *h*.

Examples: an apple, an egg, an idea, an honor, an opal

3. And connects words, phrases, and clauses. It is a coordinating connective.

Example: Don and I are going to the concert.

10.2 *Accept/Except*

1. <u>Accept</u> is a verb. It means to receive gladly, to agree to.

Example: I <u>accept</u> your invitation with pleasure.

2. <u>Except</u> is a preposition. It means excluding, but.

Example: Everyone was here <u>except</u> Jerry.

EXERCISE 10.1

Fill in the blanks with the correct words:

1. Please _____ my apology.

2. Marilyn cleaned every room in the house _____ the bathroom.

10.3 *Advice / Advise*

1. <u>Advice</u> is a noun. It means an opinion, from one not immediately concerned, about what could or should be done about a problem.

Example: Sally loves to give <u>advice</u> to everyone.

2. <u>Advise</u> is a verb. It means to offer advice; to counsel. Note: Pronounce the *s* like a *z*.

Example: My counselor <u>advised</u> me to petition for graduation soon.

EXERCISE 10.2

Fill in the blanks with the correct words:

1. Can the professor _____ me what courses to take next semester?

2. Will you follow his _____ ?

10.4   *Affect / Effect*

1. <u>Affect</u> is usually used as a verb. It means to have an influence on; to touch or move the emotions of someone.

Example: We have learned that using drugs <u>affects</u> our health.

2. <u>Effect</u> is usually used as a noun. It means the final result; the outcome.

Example: The <u>effect</u> of a drug on the nervous system is quickly observed.

EXERCISE 10.3

Fill in the blanks with the correct words:

1. The recent cold weather _____ the fruit crop.

2. The _____ of the budget cut was felt by all the employees.

10.5   *Already / All Ready*

1. <u>Already</u> is an adverb. It means by this time; before; previously.

Example: I have <u>already</u> eaten lunch, thank you.

2. <u>All ready</u> is an adjective. It is used to express complete readiness.

Example: The tourists were <u>all ready</u> to board the plane.

EXERCISE 10.4

Fill in the blanks with the correct words:

1. Everyone is _____ to go to the beach.

2. The students had _____ studied for the test.

10.6 *Dessert / Desert*

1. <u>Dessert</u> is a noun. It means the last course of a lunch or a dinner.

Example: My favorite <u>dessert</u> is apple pie.

2. <u>Desert</u> is used as a noun to mean barren land, an area of little rainfall.

Example: There is a large <u>desert</u> in Africa.

3. <u>Desert</u> is used as a verb to mean to leave or abandon.

Example: The soldier <u>deserted</u> his post during the battle.

EXERCISE 10.5

Fill in the blanks with the correct words:

1. Maria prepared fried bananas for _____.

2. Many flowers bloom in the _____ in the spring.

3. James's father _____ his family.

10.7   *Its / It's*

1. Its is the possessive form of the pronoun it.

Example: The cat licked its fur.

2. It's is the contraction of it is or it has.

Example: It's time to eat.

Many writers are tempted to add 's to the pronoun it to form the possessive. To avoid this error, read it's as it is whenever you see it to ensure that you are using the contraction of it is rather than the possessive of it, which should always be its.

EXERCISE 10.6

Fill in the blanks with the correct words:

1. _____ been raining all day.

2. The bear stuck _____ paw into the beehive.

10.8   *Know / No*

1. Know is a verb. It means to understand; to be familiar with; to be certain of.

© 1994 HarperCollins College Publishers

Example: Ed <u>knows</u> where Angie lives.

2. <u>No</u> is a negative. It means not any; not one.

Example: You have <u>no</u> reason to stay in bed today.

EXERCISE 10.7

Fill in the blanks with the correct words:

1. Some professors _____ their students well.

2. Lisa has _____ more money in her wallet.

10.9   *Lead / Led*

1. <u>Lead</u> is a noun. It is pronounced like *led*. It means a soft, bluish white element used in pencils. If it is used as a verb, it is pronounced "leed." It means to show the way by going in advance; to conduct.

Examples: <u>Lead</u> is a dense metal.
            The conductor will <u>lead</u> the orchestra.

2. <u>Led</u> is the past tense and past participle of the verb <u>lead</u>.

Example: The guide <u>led</u> us out of the forest.

EXERCISE 10.8

Fill in the blanks with the correct words:

1. Early alchemists tried to make gold out of _____ .

2. The sergeant _____ his men into battle.

10.10 *Loose / Lose*

1. <u>Loose</u> is an adjective. It means not tight fitting; too large; not fastened.

Example: The string on that package is too <u>loose</u>.

2. <u>Lose</u> is a verb. Pronounce the *s* like a *z*. It means to misplace; to fail to win.

Example: I hope my horse won't <u>lose</u> the race.

EXERCISE 10.9

Fill in the blanks with the correct words:

1. I will _____ the key if I don't buy a new key ring.

2. Linda likes to wear _____ slippers on her feet.

10.11 *Past / Passed*

1. <u>Past</u> is a noun. It means the time before the present. It can be used as an adjective to describe that which has already occurred.

Example: Try not to think about the <u>past</u>.

2. <u>Passed</u> is the past tense and past participle form of the verb <u>pass</u>. It means succeeded in, handed in, or went by.

Examples: Andrea waved and smiled as she <u>passed</u> by us.
Larry <u>passed</u> in his term paper on time.

EXERCISE 10.10

Fill in the blanks with the correct words:

1. Henry liked to tell us about his _____ experiences.

2. Tom _____ by our house last night about this time.

10.12 *Personal / Personnel*

1. Personal is an adjective. It means something private or one's own. Pronounce this word with the accent on the first syllable.

Example: My diary is my personal property.

2. Personnel is a noun. It means the group of people employed by a business or service. Pronounce this word with the accent on the last syllable. It may take either a singular or a plural verb.

Example: The president of the company sent a memo to all of the personnel.

EXERCISE 10.11

Fill in the blanks with the correct words:

1. Please don't ask so many _____ questions.

2. She was vice-president in charge of _____ in our company.

10.13   *Principal / Principle*

1. Principal is usually used as a noun. It means a person who is a leader, someone who is in charge. When it is used as an adjective, it means leading or chief.

Example: The principal of the high school spoke at the assembly.

2. Principle is a noun. It refers to basic truths, rules of human conduct, and fundamental laws.

Example: Our constitution is based on the principles of democracy.

EXERCISE 10.12

Fill in the blanks with the correct words:

1. I know him to be a man of high _____ .

2. The _____ partner in the law firm signed the contract.

10.14   *Quiet / Quite*

1. Quiet means silent, free of noise.

Example: I need a quiet place to study.

2. Quite means entirely, really, rather.

Example: You have been quite busy all day.

EXERCISE 10.13

Fill in the blanks with the correct words:

1. The Smith family live on a very _____ street.

2. The street is not _____ as _____ as it used to be.

10.15   *Suppose / Supposed*

Suppose is a verb. It means to assume to be true; to guess; to think.

Example: Do you suppose it will rain today?

Note: The verb suppose is often used in the passive and is followed by *to*. Do not forget to add the **d** to the verb: supposed.

Supposed to, in this sense, means to expect or require.

Example: He is supposed to go to the store.

The example means that he is expected to go to the store.

EXERCISE 10.14

Fill in the blanks with the correct words:

1. This is _____ to be one of the best restaurants in town.

2. I _____ we will arrive home by noon.

10.16   *Then / Than*

1. <u>Then</u> is an adverb. It means at that time; next in time, space, or order.

Example: Rhonda <u>then</u> decided to leave.

2. <u>Than</u> is used in comparative statements to introduce the second item.

Example: This suitcase is heavier <u>than</u> that one.

EXERCISE 10.15

Fill in the blanks with the correct words:

1. First we ate dinner, and _____ we went to the concert.

2. Mike gets up earlier _____ Jay does.

10.17   *There / Their / They're*

1. <u>There</u> shows direction. It means at that place. It is often used to introduce a thought, as in <u>there</u> is or <u>there</u> are.

Example: Put the tape recorder over <u>there</u>.

2. <u>Their</u> is the possessive form of the pronoun <u>they</u>. It means belonging to them.

Example: The fans received <u>their</u> tickets in the mail.

3. <u>They're</u> is a contraction of the two words <u>they are</u>.

Example: <u>They're</u> very thoughtful people.

© 1994 HarperCollins College Publishers

Fill in the blanks with the correct words:

1. I hear that _____ giving a party in _____ new home.

2. _____ is going to be a parade on St. Patrick's Day.

10.18   Through / Though / Thought

1. Through means finished. It also means to go in one side and out the other.

Examples: He is through with his work.
We walked through the park after dark.

2. Though means the same as although; despite the fact that.

Example: Though Jim had left home early, he arrived at work late.

3. Thought is the past tense and the past participle of think. It can also be used as a noun, and it means an idea.

Example: I thought you had gone home.

Fill in the blanks with the correct words:

1. I _____ you drove to New England last year.

2. _____ I closed the door quickly, the cat ran _____ it.

10.19   *To / Two / Too*

1. <u>To</u> means in the direction of, when it is used as a preposition.

Example: Pierre is going <u>to</u> Canada this summer.

Sometimes the word <u>to</u> is the first word in a verbal phrase.

Example: We are going <u>to move</u> to a new apartment next month.

2. <u>Two</u> is the same as the number 2.

Example: "You have <u>two</u> phone messages," Selena told her boyfriend.

3. <u>Too</u> means also; in addition to; very; overly so.

Example: The soup was <u>too</u> hot to eat.

EXERCISE 10.18

Fill in the blanks with the correct words:

1. _____ of the masked men approached the bank teller.

2. This dress is _____ old _____ wear _____ the party.

10.20   *Use / Used*

1. <u>Use</u> is a verb. It means to employ; to make use of. Pronounce the *s* like *z*.

Example: We <u>use</u> a broom to sweep the floor.

© 1994 HarperCollins College Publishers

2. Used is often followed by the word *to*. It means accustomed to; familiar with; was in the habit of.

Example: Selma was used to working eight hours a day.

Fill in the blanks with the correct words:

1. John is not _____ to staying up late.

2. Accountants _____ adding machines often.

10.21 Weather/ Whether

1. Weather is a noun. It refers to the state of the atmosphere at a given time or place.

Example: The weather in Kansas City is usually cold in December.

2. Whether is a subordinator. It means if it is so that; if it is the case that; in case; either.

Examples: We should find out whether the museum is open on Sundays.
He passed the test, whether by skill or luck.

Fill in the blanks with the correct words:

1. Airline pilots frequently check the _____ conditions along the route.

2. Rosetta did not know _____ to laugh or to cry.

10.22   *Whose / Who's*

1. Whose is the possessive form of the pronoun <u>who</u>. It means belonging to whom.

Example: <u>Whose</u> tennis shoes are these?

2. <u>Who's</u> is a contraction of the two words <u>who is</u>.

Example: <u>Who's</u> that man over there?

EXERCISE 10.21

Fill in the blanks with the correct words:

1. Tanya is someone _____ never at a loss for words.

2. I don't know _____ book is on the table.

10.23   *Your / You're*

1. <u>Your</u> is the possessive form of the pronoun *you*. It means belonging to you.

Example: <u>Your</u> car is in the parking lot.

2. <u>You're</u> is the contraction of the two words <u>you are</u>.

Example: <u>You're</u> going to enjoy this book, Lorraine.

EXERCISE 10.22

Fill in the blanks with the correct words:

1. _____ going to the concert with us tomorrow.

2. You bought _____ ticket a few weeks ago.

Answer Key

Chapter 1

Exercise 1.1

   X **N**   **N** **X**   **N**   **X**   **N**
1. on, highway 2. Rain, last 3. drivers, cautious 4. surface,
 N   **N**   **N**
road 5. Buick, brakes

Exercise 1.2

         N   **N**   **N**
1. Mr. Cuadros gave us two free tickets to the basketball game.
                N   **N**   **N**
2. Would you like a bowl of chicken soup and a fresh fruit salad?
             N   **N**   **N**
3. I bought a digital watch for thirty dollars at the K-Mart.
 N   **N**   **N**
4. Lori wore a new green wool dress to her job interview.
           N   **N**   **N**
5. The young doctor had a pleasant smile and a reassuring manner.

Exercise 1.3

1. dogs 2. dates 3. tricks 4. tests 5. sales 6. words
7. sentences 8. paragraphs 9. operators 10. students

Exercise 1.4

1. skies 2. days 3. ladies 4. penalties 5. keys 6. turkeys
7. counties 8. candies 9. armies 10. batteries

Exercise 1.5

1. brushes   2. watches   3. buses   4. waltzes   5. taxes
6. glasses   7. boxes   8. messes   9. rashes   10. stitches

Exercise 1.6

1. selves   2. halves   3. hooves or hoofs   4. shelves   5. proofs
6. lives   7. thieves   8. wolves   9. cliffs   10. wives

Exercise 1.7

1. sopranos   2. vetoes   3. tomatoes   4. potatoes   5. pianos
6. radios   7. zeros or zeroes   8. ratios   9. heroes   10. dominos or
dominoes

Exercise 1.8

1. mice   2. teeth   3. women   4. children   5. men

Exercise 1.9

1. the cats' names   2. their owners' commands   3. the baby's crib
4. the baby's mother   5. Ginny's food

Exercise 1.10

1. Saturday's   2. weeks'   3. Year's   4. day's   5. penny's

Exercise 1.11

1. no apostrophe   2. friends'   3. refugees'   4. no apostrophe
5. no apostrophe   6. students'   7. no apostrophe   8. customer's
or customers'   9. parents'   10. no apostrophe

Exercise 1.12

1. I enjoy eating out instead of cooking at home. Living in Seattle, I have a
choice of many different kinds of restaurants. My favorite restaurant is a Japanese one near my home. It is very small and very popular, so I usually have
to wait for a table.
2. If a person wants to learn to play a musical instrument well, he or she will
have to develop self-discipline. The serious music student, for example, must
be willing to give up watching two or three hours of television a day and, instead, spend his or her time practicing.

3. During the past year or two, the price of food has risen sharply. Every time I go to the market, you can see increases in several items. Not so long ago, your twenty dollars bought quite a few bags of groceries, but now I can carry twenty dollars' worth of food home in one bag.

4. I received a camera for a graduation present last year. It worked fine at first, but after a few months, I could tell that something was wrong with it. The pictures were so blurry that I couldn't recognize the people in them. The repairperson at the camera shop wanted too much money to repair it, so I stopped using it. I would be wasting my money to buy film for that lemon.

5. My brother likes his job as a lifeguard at the beach. He doesn't have to wear a coat and tie to work, and he is out in the fresh air all day. He has an important job. He doesn't just watch pretty girls; he is responsible for the lives of all the people who come to enjoy the ocean.

Exercise 1.13

1. theirs   2. hers   3. theirs   4. his   5. mine

Exercise 1.14

1. You're   2. They're   3. Who's   4. It's   5. They're   6. hers
7. theirs   8. its, your   9. Whose   10. You're

Exercise 1.15

1. C   2. I   3. C   4. me   5. C

Chapter 2

Exercise 2.1

1. stops, stopped   2. hurries, hurried   3. trips, tripped   4. glare, glared   5. watches, watched

Exercise 2.2

1. plans   2. works   3. saves   4. opens   5. watches
6. waits   7. listens   8. changes   9. snows   10. removes

Exercise 2.3

1. met   2. came   3. gave   4. made   5. threw
6. rode   7. ate   8. had   9. held   10. kept

Exercise 2.4

1. letting   2. jumping   3. hitting   4. returning
5. swimming   6. occurring   7. dripping   8. wrapping
9. screaming   10. getting

Exercise 2.5

1. stops, stopped, stopped, stopping   2. carries, carried, carried,
carrying   3. watches, watched, watched, watching   4. tries, tried, tried,
trying   5. hopes, hoped, hoped, hoping

Exercise 2.6

1. is, was/were, been, being   2. freezes, froze, frozen, freezing
3. runs, ran, run, running   4. chooses, chose, chosen, choosing
5. shakes, shook, shaken, shaking

Exercise 2.7

1. Do shop   2. might have received   3. have found   4. could send
5. can order

Exercise 2.8

1. have been helped   2. can see   3. can examine   4. may be done
5. must cut

Exercise 2.9

1. run   2. sung   3. seen   4. heard   5. broken
6. known   7. flown   8. brought   9. eaten   10. said

Exercise 2.10

1. is(n't)   2. should (always) practice   3. must (certainly) give   4. may
travel   5. could close

Exercise 2.11

1. will want   2. will earn   3. will begin   4. will stay   5. will ask

Exercise 2.12

1. will   2. would   3. will   4. would   5. will   6. would

Exercise 2.13

1. has, predicted   2. have, kept   3. have, planned   4. have, brought
5. have, bought

Exercise 2.14

1. had shown   2. had promised   3. had had   4. had run   5. had
chosen

Exercise 2.15

1. will have learned   2. will have paid   3. will have lived   4. will have
gone   5. will have spoken

Exercise 2.16

1. Last Tuesday night I went to the library because I had a test in history on
Wednesday morning. It was too noisy at home to study. My brother was playing the stereo, my mother was vacuuming, and my little sister and her friend
were chasing each other around the house. How was I supposed to concentrate with all that commotion?
2. My friend Greg loves peanut butter. Every morning he spreads peanut
butter on his toast or waffles. He snacks on peanut butter cups at school,
and, of course, he eats peanut butter sandwiches for lunch every day. Nowa-
days, he bakes his own peanut butter cookies because his mother has refused
to make them anymore. Greg is a hopeless case; he even covers a slice of
chocolate cake with peanut butter.
3. My wife and I bought a golden retriever puppy last year. We made the
mistake on the first few nights of allowing the puppy to sleep on a rug by our
bed because he missed his brothers and sisters. Later when we made a bed
for him in the laundry room, he howled and scratched on the door for several hours every night. After a while the neighbors called on the telephone
to complain about the noise. We thought that he would never give up. The
puppy finally learned to sleep by himself, and the neighbors started speaking
to us again.

Chapter 3

Exercise 3.1

Subject	Auxiliary Verb	Main Verb
1. Scotsman	Does	wear
2. Americans	can	satisfy
3. festivals	are	held
4. events	———	include
5. contestants	are	throwing

Exercise 3.2

The following are possible responses:

1. Come   2. Put   3. Shut   4. Meet   5. Get

Exercise 3.3

1. [Since 1789], [between the ages], [of fourteen and eighteen], [as congressional pages], [in our nation's capital]
2. [during vacation], [in Washington, D.C.], [for a year], [at Page School], [in the Library of Congress]
3. [for members], [of Congress], [from 9 A.M.], [to 5 P.M.]
4. [of the present system], [at home], [with their parents]
5. [despite the pressures], [of a busy schedule], [of national political life]

Exercise 3.4

1. [on top of the car], [of luggage]   2. [instead of a salad], [with his dinner]
3. [in front of me], [about the long wait], [in line]   4. [After two innings], [at Yankee Stadium], [because of rain]   5. [together with several council members], [in a panel discussion], [on the city's transit problems]

Exercise 3.5

Subject	Verb	Direct Object
1. uncle	plays	———
2. children	asked	questions

© 1994 HarperCollins College Publishers

3. you   did order   food _____
4. Marilyn   sang   ———————
5. Steve   can play   guitar

Exercise 3.6

        S   LV   C
1. My (daughter) is a first-year student at Jackson Community College.
      S   LV   C
2. (Everyone) seemed happy about the election results.
                 S   Aux   LV   C
3. The traffic (light) is finally turning green.
     S   S   Aux   LV   C
4. (Mario and Kevin) have just become partners.
   Aux   S   LV   C
5. Can (you) be the moderator of our next discussion?

Exercise 3.7

1. He, it   2. you, she   3. you, we   4. They   5. I

Exercise 3.8

1. it   2. us   3. her   4. you, them   5. me

Exercise 3.9

1. him   2. He, I   3. us   4. I   5. he, I

Exercise 3.10

1. she'll   2. they've   3. he'd   4. he's   5. I'll   6. I'm   7. we've
8. here's   9. it's   10. we're

Exercise 3.11

Your sentences will vary.

1. S-LV-NC   2. S-V-O   3. S-V   4. S-V-O   5. S-V   6. S-LV-AC
7. S-V   8. S-LV-NC   9. S-V-O   10. S-LV-AC

Chapter 4

Exercise 4.1

1. New York City's, its   2. His, city's   3. Today's, America's
4. salt's, our   5. engineer's, people's

Exercise 4.2

1. box, fought   2. turning, home   3. winning, rookie, head
4. excited, place, goal   5. winning, laughing, shouting, football

Exercise 4.3

It is [a] [beautiful] [sunny] day in [a] [popular] [theme] park in [the] United
States. Mr. and Mrs. Tomita on [their] [first] trip to [this] country, listen attentively to [a] [tour] [guide's] claim that [thirty-five thousand] adults and
children visit [the] park [every] day. [Most] visitors to [this] [magical] place
are [attracted] by [an] [amazing] variety of shows, rides, exhibits, and restaurants. [Both] Mr. and Mrs. Tomita, however, are impressed by [the] [clean]
surroundings. They are staying at [the] [vacation-land's] hotel where [all]
[the] rooms have immaculately [clean] [blue] [plastic] furniture, [green] and
[beige] walls, and beds [covered] with [purple-green] spreads. [The] [hotel's]
[parking] lot, with [its] carefully [planted] vegetation, is also sparkling [clean.]
[The] [smallest] scrap of litter is sucked underground and rushed via pipes to
[a] [fabulous] [trash] compactor. Even [the] [friendly] birds do [their] part by
picking [some] [bread] crumbs off [the] [restaurant's] patio at [the] hotel. Mr.
and Mrs. Tomita know that they will enjoy themselves in [this] [spotless]
[American] [tourist] attraction.

Exercise 4.4

1. cluttered, noisy   2. frigid, ice-covered   3. battered, rusty; luxurious,
shiny   4. graceful, elegant   5. old-fashioned, clumsy, worn-out

Exercise 4.5

1. less interesting   2. least dangerous   3. less expensive   4. least
creative   5. less sleepy

Exercise 4.6

1. most important   2. easier   3. better   4. bigger, more powerful
5. most recent   6. greater   7. more efficient   8. simpler *or* more
simple   9. largest   10. best, lowest

Exercise 4.7

The following are possible sentences.

1. Kimiko arrived at 8:00 o'clock after a long flight from Tokyo.
2. The pilot landed the plane smoothly and silently.
3. All the passengers on the plane applauded loudly.
4. Kimiko walked quickly toward the exit door to deplane.
5. She was thrilled to be in Chicago after so many years.

Exercise 4.8

1. most reluctantly   2. less efficiently   3. more systematically
4. most definitely   5. more easily

Exercise 4.9

1. Today 1,500 Seminole (Indians) live [on the reservation built on 120,000 acres of swamp in the Florida Everglades.]

2. A (group) [of these Indians, living near Tampa,] has defied the law.

3. [In addition to a shrine and a museum,] the (Seminoles) have built a drive-thru smoke shop there.

4. The (Indians) have been selling cigarettes [without charging sales tax.]

5. [From the first,] state and local law (enforcers) did not like these Indians [to sell cigarettes.]

Exercise 4.10

1. profit, Carolyn   2. time, Josephine   3. mountains, we
4. shoes, Tina   5. school, Jerry

Exercise 4.11

1. Nick saved almost $100 by making his own repairs on his car.

2. The candidate promised at the political rally that he would reduce unemployment.

3. Alfredo ordered a pizza with mushrooms and pepperoni to go.

4. The painters told us on Wednesday that they would begin painting the house.

or The painters told us that they would begin painting the house on Wednesday.

5. Rex suddenly saw a woman in the front row jump up and run out . . . exit.

or Rex . . . jump up suddenly . . . exit.

Exercise 4.12

The following is a possible revision. Yours may vary.

Expecting a robot like R2D2, Willy was disappointed by the robot that was demonstrated to him. Willy had hoped the robot would have useful arms and legs, but it propelled itself on large wheels. Having limited mobility, the robot could not climb stairs. A distance of less than seventy feet was necessary between the robot and its owner for the robot to be able to respond to voice commands. Frustrated by the poor quality, Willy decided to delay his decision to buy a robot.

Chapter 5

Exercise 5.1

1. main clause   2. main clause   3. phrase   4. phrase   5. phrase

Exercise 5.2

Subject	Auxiliary Verb	Verb	Type of Sentence
1. people	—	think	
bicyclists	—	know	compound
2. bicyclists	—	ride	simple
3. ride	—	begins	
it	—	ends	compound
4. riders	—	complain	simple
5. bicyclists	are	surprised	
land	had	looked	compound

Exercise 5.3

1. The (doctor) was a well-known specialist, but my (father) would not accept her diagnosis.
2. The pole (vaulter) tried again to break the record, and this time (he) succeeded.
3. (It) is a large house, so (they) will have room for all their furniture.
4. (Andrea) spent four hours a day practicing the flute, for (she) was determined to improve.
5. (We) can drive to the beach, or (we) can ride our bicycles.

Exercise 5.4

1. (Lucy) likes to finish her homework before dinner; after
   eating (she) gets sleepy.   C
2. (Vivian) brought pictures of our high-school class to the
   reunion; (everyone) laughed at the dated clothes and
   hairstyles.   C
3. (Arturo) and his (brother) have borrowed money and
   opened a real estate office.   S
4. Our (neighbor) was happy about his golf game today; for
   the first time (he) had a lower score than his wife's. (or:
   game; today)   C
5. The (children) entertained themselves for half an hour by
   riding up and down on the escalator.   S

Exercise 5.5

1. (We) had planned to bicycle through England last summer; instead, (we) painted the house and built a fence.
2. (I) forgot my umbrella this morning; consequently, (I) was soaked to the skin by the time (I) reached the office.
3. (Milt) works six hours a day and overtime on weekends at a restaurant; in addition, (he) takes three classes at a community college.

4. First (Norman) reads the comics; then, (he) settles down to enjoy the sports section.

5. (Cindy) looked very different with her new haircut; in fact, (I) hardly recognized her.

Exercise 5.6

1. Besides that, a   2. dictionary, in addition, shows   3. you, furthermore, the   4. dictionary, in fact, is   5. You must, however, develop

Exercise 5.7

1. gardener, secretary, short-order cook
2. giving information, keeping the park, and preserving the natural beauty
3. puts on her uniform, packs her lunch, and rides her bicycle
4. Most faces are new, but others are familiar.
5. sunny or rainy, sizzling or freezing
6. to enjoy nature and to hike in the woods
7. Dedicated and enthusiastic
8. answering questions and being helpful

Exercise 5.8

1. sand, pebbles, rocks, and acrylic paint
2. Venezuela, Argentina, Peru, Chile, and Brazil
3. bath, went . . . room, closed . . . door, turned . . . radio, and lay . . . bed
4. to clean, to cook, to iron, or to shop
5. flying hand gliders, going deep-sea fishing, or riding horseback

Exercise 5.9

1. The (children) ran around the park; their (mothers) tried to quiet them unsuccessfully.   FS
2. The (traffic) was unusually heavy this evening; (it) was caused by an accident at the intersection.   CS
3. The (smog) disappeared after the heavy rains; (it) reappeared in a few days.   FS
4. In the early morning, many (joggers) are running.   NE
5. (It) was late, and all the (lights) in the house were out.   NE

Exercise 5.10

The following are possible revisions. Your sentences may vary.

1. More corporations are beginning to open day-care centers for their employees' children; the centers are open from nine to five.
2. Working parents take fewer days off if their children are well cared for because they worry less.
3. Two-paycheck families appreciate the cost benefits, for the price of a full-time babysitter would use up an entire salary.
4. Single-parent families especially appreciate the convenience of quality child-care programs; in fact, child-care programs help to recruit high-quality employees.
5. Government support helps the corporations build special facilities; pre-school playgrounds and indoor classrooms are often too expensive for smaller corporations to construct.

Chapter 6

Exercise 6.1

1. The (guests) left (after) the (party) was over.
2. The (animals) performed their tricks (although) the (audience) did not applaud.
3. (When) the (instructor) passed back our papers, (I) was delighted.
4. Mr. (Hashimoto) has been wearing a cast (because) (he) broke his leg.
5. (While) (we) were riding our bicycles, (someone) stole our car.

Exercise 6.2

1. After dinner, (while) the (guests) sat around the table, (many) of them told interesting stories about their work (as) (we) all listened attentively.
2. (Although) (she) said (that) (she) loved him, (he) didn't believe her (because) (he) knew (that) (she) went out with many other men.
3. (As long as) (you) haven't eaten your lunch yet, (you) might as well wait until dinner time (when) (we) will have a big meal.

4. (Before) Ⓘ knew (ⓦhat) was <u>happening</u>, the red sports Ⓒar <u>passed</u> my car (as) Ⓘ <u>drove</u> up the hill.

5. The Ⓙudge <u>said</u> (that) Ⓘ <u>should go</u> to driving school (so that) Ⓘ <u>would learn</u> about the <u>dangers</u> of drunk driving.

Exercise 6.3

1. His lifetime batting record, which remained unbroken until the summer of 1985, was 4,191 hits in 24 seasons.
2. Cobb, who was a millionaire, gave . . .
3. Since most of his fans were ignorant of his violent disposition, he remained . . .
4. He welcomed a fight even when he was sick and old.
5. Cobb threatened to use a loaded handgun that he carried with him.

Exercise 6.4

1. The coach was fired because his team never won a game.
2. When the cat dug holes in my flower beds, I chased it away.
3. Although they lost the first game, they won the second one.
4. While we were riding our bicycles, someone stole our car.
5. Toni, who is a full-time college student, works thirty hours a week as a musician.

Exercise 6.5

1. dog, which is a poodle, digs
2. no comma
3. Mary, which . . . liner, is
4. stereo, which . . . ours, has
5. no comma

Exercise 6.6

The following are possible sentences. Your sentences may vary.

1. Michelle has completed almost all the courses required by her major, except for English 1, Psychology 2, and History 17.
2. Shelby has big plans for the sweepstakes money if he wins it. For example, he hopes to travel to many foreign countries, including several in Africa.

3. This fabric offers a number of advantages for traveling in the summer, such as being washable, quick-drying, wrinkle-free, and lightweight.
4. She passed the time on jury duty by knitting and by working crossword puzzles.
5. The instructor reviewed the material to be covered in the chapter test and especially called our attention to the last three pages.

Exercise 6.7

1. S   2. S   3. F   4. F   5. F   6. F   7. S   8. F   9. F   10. F

Chapter 7

Exercise 7.1

1. tree	gives
2. student	likes
3. photograph	is
4. driver	collects
5. car	requires

Exercise 7.2

Subjects	Aux. Verbs and Main Verbs	Words Between Subject and Verb
1. purpose	is	(of many zoos in large cities)
2. visitors	were	(to the zoo, not the animals)
3. animal	spends	(in one of these new zoos no longer)
4. quarters	give	(like those in San Diego's Wild Animal Park)
5. keepers	work	(whenever possible)

Exercise 7.3

Subject	Verb
1. disagreement	is
2. much	is
3. chances	are
4. clue	is
5. humidity	signals

Exercise 7.4

1. are   2. were   3. are   4. is   5. answers

Exercise 7.5

1. taste   2. seems   3. were   4. makes   5. hears
   (cookies) (president) (sisters) (bottle) (instructor)

Exercise 7.6

1. have   2. have   3. have   4. have   5. has

Exercise 7.7

1. works   2. needs   3. plans   4. spends   5. seems

Exercise 7.8

1. are   2. have   3. was   4. Is   5. was

Exercise 7.9

1. is   2. was   3. is   4. sounds   5. causes

Exercise 7.10

Antecedents	Verbs
1. Americans	seek
2. family	goes
3. recorders	plug
4. videogames	hook
5. television	has

Exercise 7.11

Pronouns	Antecedents
1. their	Tanya and Rosalie
2. his	engineer
3. your	you
4. me	I
5. they	sweaters

Exercise 7.12

Pronouns	Antecedents
1. her or his	artist
2. their	visitors
3. her	Mrs. Jones
4. they	birds
5. their	students

Exercise 7.13

Pronouns	Antecedent
1. their	Ralph or George
2. their	Mr. and Mrs. Asano
3. her	Either Martha or Angela
4. their	either gardener or window cleaners
5. his	Neither Bruce nor Richard

Exercise 7.14

1. its   2. their   3. its   4. their   5. its

Exercise 7.15

Pronouns	Antecedents
1. his or her	Someone
2. his or her	anyone
3. her	each
4. his or her	Nobody
5. his or her	Everyone

Exercise 7.16

1. who   2. that   3. who   4. that   5. that

Exercise 7.17

1. who   2. whom   3. who   4. whom   5. who

Exercise 7.18

1. Marla said to Tess, "I have lost my pen."

2. There are so many automobile accidents because drivers are careless.

3. Dr. Bronowski is a great surgeon. Surgery is a rewarding profession.

4. Before taking a test, Roberto studies and gets a good night's sleep. Rest is important.

5. The graduates marched solemnly down the aisle to receive their diplomas. The ceremony was so inspiring.

Chapter 8

Exercise 8.1

1. Andrew did not want to wear his raincoat to school yesterday, nor did he want to carry an umbrella.

2. I have seen that movie star before, yet I cannot remember her name.

3. Louis and Gerald tried out for the basketball team, and both of them were chosen.

4. Brett and Lula were married on Friday morning, but they did not leave for Hawaii until Saturday.

5. Athletes must train hard and watch their diets every day, or they will not be able to compete.

Exercise 8.2

1. No   2. No   3. No   4. No   5. Yes

Exercise 8.3

1. Last semester Evelyn took four classes at college, worked twenty hours a week and sang in the church choir on weekends. (*or* week, and)

2. My favorite breakfast cereal contains the following ingredients: malt, barley, oats, honey, and raisins.

3. He caught the pass, ran along the sideline for twenty yards into the end zone but failed to score because he had stepped out of bounds on the two-yard line. (*or* zone, but)

4. The students were told to bring their workbooks, dictionaries, lined paper, and pens to every class meeting.

5. The recipe listed the following ingredients: sugar, butter, flour, cocoa, walnuts, milk, and peanut butter.

Exercise 8.4

1. Yes   2. No   3. Yes   4. No   5. Yes

© 1994 HarperCollins College Publishers

Exercise 8.5

1. Within two or three months, the parking lot will be less crowded.
2. After a short pause, the speaker answered the questions from the audience.
3. Best of all, the food is always served hot.
4. In many tropical countries, the natives take a siesta in the middle of the day.
5. John has been commuting twenty-five miles a day to school. Fortunately, he found an apartment for rent near the college yesterday.

Exercise 8.6

1. No   2. No   3. Yes   4. Yes   5. No

Exercise 8.7

1. Although Jo Ellen had always known the truth about Harry, she still loved him.
2. Before you can understand calculus, you must understand algebra and trigonometry.
3. If the rain doesn't stop soon, the rivers will overflow their banks.
4. By the time you are ready to take the test, you will be able to answer all of the questions correctly.
5. The thick salmon steak was delicious even though it was a little overcooked.

Exercise 8.8

1. No   2. Yes   3. Yes   4. No   5. Yes

Exercise 8.9

1. The raindrops fell into the clear, blue, deep water of the pool.
2. Shana left her discarded, smelly clothes scattered around her large, sunlit bedroom.
3. The acrobat entertained the huge, enthusiastic audience by his skillful, graceful performance.
4. In the early morning, the joggers run effortlessly along the deserted, shell-strewn beach.
5. Marge's pink sunburnt skin looked painful to me.

Exercise 8.10

1. No   2. No   3. No   4. Yes   5. No

Exercise 8.11

1. We hope, therefore, that you will send our refund soon.
2. Karen's parents, as a rule, drive her to school every day.
3. The jury, as a result, took four days to arrive at the verdict.
4. The kitchen, in fact, has not been cleaned since last week.
5. My opinion, in the long run, is based on the facts as I understand them.

Exercise 8.12

1. Yes   2. No   3. No   4. No   5. No

Exercise 8.13

1. I don't entirely agree, Jim, with your position.
2. Play it again, Sam.
3. Ladies and gentlemen of the jury, you have heard the evidence.
4. Ella, tell me that you love me.
5. I hope, Paulette, that you will practice your lesson.

Exercise 8.14

1. No   2. Yes   3. No   4. No   5. Yes

Exercise 8.15

1. My friend Carla Caraway went to New York to get a job as a dancer.
2. A young woman, alone in a strange city, must learn how to take care of herself.
3. She auditioned for Judith Jamison, the famous choreographer of the Alvin Ailey company.
4. Carla, breathless and exhausted, waited after the audition to hear the choreographer's opinion.
5. Carla joined the Ailey company, one of the best dance companies in the world.

Exercise 8.16

1. Yes   2. No   3. Yes   4. No   5. No

Exercise 8.17

1. A talented American contralto, Marian Anderson, who had sung at the White House, was barred from singing in Constitution Hall in Washington.
2. Instead, Ms. Anderson sang at the Lincoln Memorial before 75,000 people who had gathered in support of her.
3. Three Aaron Copland ballets, drawing upon American themes, are *Billy the Kid, Rodeo,* and *Appalachian Spring.*
4. Copland wrote *Appalachian Spring* for Martha Graham, choreographer and dancer.
5. Ernest Hemingway, an American author, began his first job as a newspaper reporter at the age of eighteen.

Exercise 8.18

1. "I can never do these homework assignments," Gary complained.
2. "Well," said his mother, "you haven't even tried."
3. "I never learn anything in that class," he said, "so what's the point?"
4. "Besides," he said to her, "I have a date tonight."
5. "Gary, you should do your assignment before you go out," his mother advised.

Exercise 8.19

1. George will move to Las Vegas, Nevada, in January.
2. His address has been The Stanford Arms Hotel, Apt. 10, 536 W. 18th Street, Rittman, Indiana 46206, for the last six years.
3. We will forward his mail to his new address: The Pyramid Hotel, Las Vegas, Nevada 89501.
4. The Battle of Gettysburg was fought on July 4, 1863.
5. The annual rodeo in Palmdale, California, features a bull-riding contest.

Exercise 8.20

1. No 2. Yes 3. Yes 4. No 5. Yes

Chapter 9

Exercise 9.1

1. When did you last study punctuation?
2. Mr. Newman is a famous actor.

3. Help! Fire!
4. I would be living in New York if I could afford an apartment on E. 68th Street.
5. He earned his B.A. degree from NYU.
6. Hal wondered what was wrong with him.
7. What is wrong with Hal?
8. Hooray! We've won the game!
9. When we were young, we never questioned why we were poor.
10. How are you today?

Exercise 9.2

1. for; he
2. television; then
3. ingredients: flour
4. cars: an
5. Sacramento; Betty Ford, Palm Springs; and
6. library; however,
7. 3:45 P.M.; nevertheless,
8. entrees: lasagna
9. winter; therefore,
10. movie; we

Exercise 9.3

1. "The Lottery," "A Rose for Emily"
2. "Have you seen The Tempest at the Old Globe Theater yet?"
3. Beloved
4. "Stop that shoplifter!"
5. "Read . . . tomorrow"?
6. "A . . . Problem," Times
7. "The Owl and the Pussycat"
8. Cheers, Roseanne, L.A. Law
9. "Poetry and Advertising," Language in Thought and Action
10. "College Tuition," The Atlantic

Exercise 9.4

1. fifty-year-old
2. left-hand, one-way
3. dry-cleaned
4. sharp-eyed, run-down sus-

5. sister-in-law, second-hand, seventy-two
6. free-lance, self-help
7. Two-thirds, cov-, high-risk
8. bullet-scarred, high-rise
9. major-elect, upper-class, self-reliance
10. half-heartedly, self-hypnosis

Exercise 9.5

1. Anh Nguyen, American
2. I'm, English 1, I'm, History 21
3. When Mary, New York, Metropolitan Museum of Art
4. I, *Phantom of the Opera*
5. Sue's, Ritz, Kraft, Coca-Cola
6. When Darlene, Sears, Wamsutta
7. Are, Sugar Bowl, New Year's Day
8. In, I, Saturdays
9. Yellowstone National Park, United States
10. My, Hemingway, I

Chapter 10

Exercise 10.1

1. accept   2. except

Exercise 10.2

1. advise   2. advice

Exercise 10.3

1. affected   2. effect

Exercise 10.4

1. all ready   2. already

Exercise 10.5

1. dessert   2. desert   3. deserted

Exercise 10.6

1. It's   2. its

Exercise 10.7

1. know   2. no

Exercise 10.8

1. lead   2. led

Exercise 10.9

1. lose   2. loose

Exercise 10.10

1. past   2. passed

Exercise 10.11

1. personal   2. personnel

Exercise 10.12

1. principles   2. principal

Exercise 10.13

1. quiet   2. quite, quiet

Exercise 10.14

1. supposed   2. suppose

Exercise 10.15

1. then   2. than

Exercise 10.16

1. they're, their   2. There

Exercise 10.17

1. thought   2. Though, through

Exercise 10.18

1. Two   2. too, to, to

Exercise 10.19

1. used   2. use

Exercise 10.20

1. weather   2. whether

Exercise 10.21

1. who's   2. whose

Exercise 10.22

1. You're   2. your

Glossary

Action verbs tell what the subject does, did, or will do.

Adjective clauses are **subordinate clauses** that are also called **relative clauses** because the **subordinator** "relates" the rest of the subordinate clause to a **noun** or **pronoun** in the **main clause**. The subordinate clause acts like an **adjective** modifying that part of the main clause by adding information about it.

Adjectives make **nouns** or **pronouns** more specific or concrete by limiting and describing them.

Adverb clauses are **subordinate clauses** that are introduced by a **subordinator**, which specifies time, place, cause, condition, or contrast when indicating the relationship between the **main** and the **subordinate clause**.

Adverbial connectives (*however, nevertheless, then*) are words that are used with a semicolon and a comma to join **main clauses** together. They are also called **adverbial conjunctions** or **conjunctive adverbs**.

Adverbs modify **verbs, adjectives,** or other **adverbs** and answer one of the following questions: When? Why? How? Where?

Agreement is the matching in **number, gender,** and **person** between words. **Subjects** and **verbs** must agree, and **pronouns** must agree with their **antecedents**.

Antecedents are **nouns, pronouns,** or **noun phrases** to which a noun refers.

Auxiliary verbs are helping verbs used with main verbs to form **verb phrases**.

Base forms of verbs are the present forms of the verbs with no *-s* at the end.

Collective nouns (such as *family*) refer to a collection of persons, places, things, ideas, or activities.

Comma splices are grammatical errors that occur when **main clauses** are joined with only a comma and no **connectives**.

Common nouns name people, places, things, ideas, or activities in general.

Comparatives are the forms of **adjectives** or **adverbs** used to compare two people, places, ideas, things, or actions.

Completers follow **linking verbs** to describe or rename the subject.

Complex sentences are composed of a **main clause** and one or more **subordinate clauses**.

Compound antecedents are two or more **antecedents** joined by a **coordinating connective**. When joined by *and*, they require a plural pronoun. When joined by *or, neither . . . nor,* or *either . . . or,* they require a pronoun that agrees with the antecedent closer to the pronoun.

Compound objects are two or more **direct objects** joined by a **coordinating connective**.

Compound sentences contain two or more **main clauses** joined by a **connective** and by appropriate punctuation.

Compound subjects are two or more **subjects** joined by a **coordinating connective**.

Compound verbs are two or more **verbs** joined by a **coordinating connective**.

Connectives are the words used to connect words, phrases, and clauses.

Contractions are words that are formed by combining two words with an apostrophe for the omission of letters.

Coordinating connectives (*and, but, or, for, nor, so, yet*) are words used with a comma to join words, phrases, and **main clauses** together. They are also called **coordinating conjunctions**.

Dangling modifiers are **adjectives** or **adverbs** that do not modify any word in the sentence. Sentences with dangling modifiers can be rewritten by inserting a word for the modifier to limit or describe.

Direct objects are the **nouns** or **pronouns** that answer the question "What?" or "Whom?" after an **action verb**. **Objects** also follow **prepositions**.

Faulty parallelism is the failure to place similar items in similar grammatical form.

Fused sentences are grammatical errors that occur when **main clauses** are joined with no punctuation or **connectives**.

Gender indicates whether a third-person **pronoun** is masculine, feminine, or neuter.

Indefinite pronouns (such as *anyone* or *someone*) usually take a singular verb and require a singular pronoun.

Irregular verbs do not follow any spelling rules to form the past tense.

Linking verbs connect the subject to its description. Common linking verbs include *become, feel, seem, appear,* and the forms of the verb *be.*

Main clauses (also called **independent clauses**) are groups of related words with a subject and a verb that can stand alone as a sentence if the first word is capitalized and the clause ends with a mark of punctuation such as a period or a question mark.

© 1994 HarperCollins College Publishers

Misplaced modifiers are **adjectives** or **adverbs** that have been placed next to words they do not modify. They confuse the reader and should be moved closer to the words they modify.

Modifiers describe, limit, or make specific another word in the sentence.

Noun markers are **adjectives** that point to the **noun** that follows them.

Noun phrases are groups of words that include a **noun** and its **modifiers**.

Nouns name people, places, things, ideas, or activities.

Number indicates whether a **pronoun** is singular or plural.

Parallel structure is the placing of similar items in similar grammatical form.

Participles are verb forms that may function as part of a **verb phrase** (was *laughing*) or as an **adjective** (The *winning* team, *laughing* and *shouting*, ran off the field). The **present participle** is formed by adding *-ing* to the base form of the verb. The **past participle** of a regular verb is formed by adding *-d* or *-ed* to the base form.

Perfect tenses are formed by using a form of the **auxiliary verb** *have* and the **past participle** of the main verb.

Person indicates the person speaking, the person spoken to, or the person or thing spoken about.

Phrases are groups of words without a **subject** and a **verb**. Examples are **noun phrases, verb phrases,** and **prepositional phrases**.

Plural nouns refer to more than one person, place, thing, idea, or activity.

Possessive nouns are nouns that change spelling to indicate a belonging-to relationship.

Prepositions are the words used to show position, direction, or relationship.

Present participles are formed by adding *-ing* to the base form of a verb.

Pronouns are used to take the place of a **noun** or to refer to a noun. A **personal pronoun** shows **person, number,** and **gender**.

Proper nouns name specific people, places, things, ideas, or activities.

Regular verbs add *-d* or *-ed* to form the past tense.

Relative pronouns are **subordinators** (such as *who* or *which*) that introduce a **subordinate clause**. The relative pronoun must agree with the **noun** or **noun phrase** in the **main clause** as its **antecedent**.

Sentence fragments are groups of words that begin with a capital letter and end with a period, but do not express a complete thought or contain a **main clause**.

Sentences must contain at least one **subject** and one **verb** and express a complete thought.

Simple sentences are **sentences** that contain one **main clause**.

Subjects are the people or things the **verb** is asking or telling about.

Subordinate clauses (also called **dependent clauses**) are groups of related words with **subjects** and **verbs** that are introduced by a **subordinator**. They make incomplete statements, so they must be attached to a **main clause** to be a complete sentence.

Subordinators are words that are used to introduce a **subordinate clause**. Examples: *because, that, although.*

Superlatives are the forms of **adjectives** or **adverbs** used to compare three or more people, places, ideas, things, or actions.

Tense is the change of verb form to indicate when the action occurred.

Verbal phrases include a **verbal** plus a **noun** and/or a prepositional phrase. Examples: to choose a pet, choosing a pet; chosen for its intelligence.

Verbals are formed from **verbs** and are used to introduce **verbal phrases**. They include one of the three following forms: *to* plus the base form of the verb, a present participle, or a past participle.

Verbs are the words in **sentences** that indicate the action of the sentence.

Index